# OXFORD
## First
## Encyclopedia

# OXFORD
# First
# Encyclopedia

Andrew Langley

OXFORD UNIVERSITY PRESS

Oxford University Press
Great Clarendon Street
Oxford OX2 6DP

Oxford  New York  Athens  Auckland  Bangkok
Bogotá  Bombay  Buenos Aires  Calcutta
Cape Town  Dar es Salaam  Delhi  Florence
Hong Kong  Istanbul  Karachi Kuala Lumpur
Madras  Madrid  Melbourne  Mexico City  Nairobi
Paris  Singapore  Taipei  Tokyo  Toronto  Warsaw

and associated companies in Berlin  Ibadan

*Oxford* is a trade mark of Oxford University Press

A CIP catalogue record for this book
is available from the British Library

ISBN 0-19-910091-8

1 3 5 7 9 10 8 6 4 2

Printed in Spain by Graficas Estella

# Contents

## *My Body*  7

## *People and Places*  29

## *The Arts*  51

# How to use this book

The picture below shows two pages from this book.
Read all the labels around the picture carefully.
They will help you to find your way around the
book, and make using it simple and fun.

This is the title for this topic. The Contents list gives the titles for all the topics, and the pages that they are on.

On the left-hand page there is always an introduction. This is the part that you should read first.

This is an activity box. Activity boxes have ideas for things for you to do or make.

This big icon shows the section this topic is in. The name of the section is next to it – "Science".

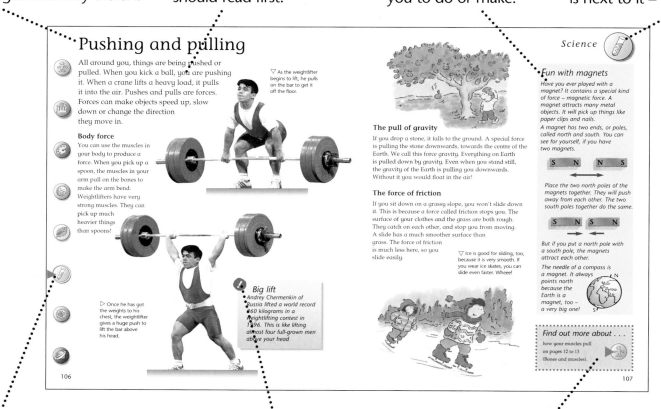

## Pushing and pulling

All around you, things are being pushed or pulled. When you kick a ball, you are pushing it. When a crane lifts a heavy load, it pulls it into the air. Pushes and pulls are forces. Forces can make objects speed up, slow down or change the direction they move in.

### Body force

You can use the muscles in your body to produce a force. When you pick up a spoon, the muscles in your arm pull on the bones to make the arm bend. Weightlifters have very strong muscles. They can pick up much heavier things than spoons!

▷ As the weightlifter begins to lift, he pulls on the bar to get it off the floor.

▷ Once he has got the weights to his chest, the weightlifter gives a huge push to lift the bar above his head.

**Big lift**
Andrey Chermenkin of Russia lifted a world record 260 kilograms in a weightlifting contest in 1996. This is like lifting almost four full-grown men above your head!

106

### The pull of gravity

If you drop a stone, it falls to the ground. A special force is pulling the stone downwards, towards the centre of the Earth. We call this force gravity. Everything on Earth is pulled down by gravity. Even when you stand still, the gravity of the Earth is pulling you downwards. Without it you would float in the air!

### The force of friction

If you sit down on a grassy slope, you won't slide down it. This is because a force called friction stops you. The surface of your clothes and the grass are both rough. They catch on each other, and stop you from moving. A slide has a much smoother surface than grass. The force of friction is much less here, so you slide easily.

▷ Ice is good for sliding, too, because it is very smooth. If you wear ice skates, you can slide even faster. Wheee!

*Science*

### Fun with magnets

Have you ever played with a magnet? It contains a special kind of force – magnetic force. A magnet attracts many metal objects. It will pick up things like paper clips and nails.
A magnet has two ends, or poles, called north and south. You can see for yourself, if you have two magnets.

| S | N | | N | S |

Place the two north poles of the magnets together. They will push away from each other. The two south poles together do the same.

| S | N | | S | N |

But if you put a north pole with a south pole, the magnets attract each other.
The needle of a compass is a magnet. It always points north because the Earth is a magnet, too – a very big one!

**Find out more about . . .**
how your muscles pull on pages 12 to 13 (Bones and muscles).

107

These pictures are called "icons". There is one for each section of the book, from "My Body" at the top, to "The Universe" at the bottom. The red triangle points to the icon for the section you are in. On this page it is pointing at the "Science" icon.

A box with an exclamation mark tells you something interesting or unusual about the topic.

The "Find out more about . . ." box tells you about other pages in the book where there is more about the topic. The icon is the one for the section where you can read more.

## The Index and Glossary

The meaning of important words used in the book is explained in the Glossary. The Glossary is near the end of the book, just before the Index. The Index tells you where to look if you want to read about a particular topic. Suppose that you want to read about giraffes. Find the letter G in the index, then look down the list until you find 'giraffe'. Next to the word is a number: 86. This tells you that there is something about giraffes on page 86.

# My Body

Your body is an amazingly complicated machine, with lots of parts working together. The fuels that keep it going are the food you eat and oxygen from the air. A machine may have hundreds, or even thousands of parts, but your body has millions and millions! Your skin, bones, muscles and all the different organs are made of tiny parts called cells. They all work together so that you can eat, sleep, breathe, run, laugh, cry, shout – and read this book!

brain

nerves

heart

lungs

liver

kidneys

stomach

intestines

head

skull

spine

arm muscles

shoulder

rib cage

pelvis

leg muscles

cell

# Look at me

Look at your face in the mirror. You can see your eyes, your ears, your nose and your mouth. Each of these features is one of your senses. We have five senses altogether – sight, hearing, smell, taste and touch. Without them, we would not know anything about the world around us.

▷ How many different ways of using the senses can you see in this picture?

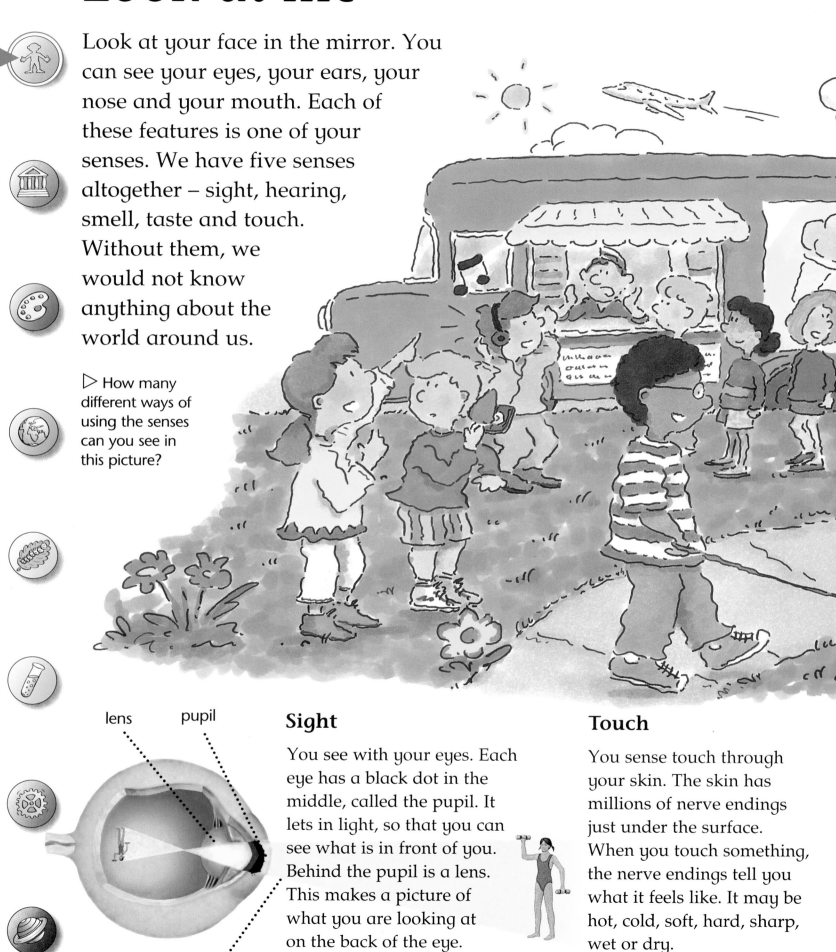

### Sight

You see with your eyes. Each eye has a black dot in the middle, called the pupil. It lets in light, so that you can see what is in front of you. Behind the pupil is a lens. This makes a picture of what you are looking at on the back of the eye.

lens    pupil

light

### Touch

You sense touch through your skin. The skin has millions of nerve endings just under the surface. When you touch something, the nerve endings tell you what it feels like. It may be hot, cold, soft, hard, sharp, wet or dry.

## Make a "feely" bag

*You use several senses to tell what things are. Try fooling your friends by only letting them use one sense: their sense of touch. Find a plastic bag (one you cannot see through), and put in some grapes with the skins peeled off. Ask your friends to guess what is in the bag by feeling. You could tell them that the grapes are eyeballs, and see what they do!*

### Sound

You hear with your ears. Sounds are vibrations in the air. The ear flaps on the outside of your head gather sounds from outside, and tiny bones inside your ear make them louder.

tiny bones

ear flap

△ You can use one sense to help you with another! Blind people cannot see. But they can read books which have a special kind of "writing" called Braille. Each letter has a code of dots. These dots are printed so that they stick up slightly from the page, and readers can feel them with their fingers.

## Smell and taste

You smell with your nose and taste with your tongue. Smells in the air come in through your nose as you breathe. Your tongue is covered in tiny bumps called taste buds. These tell you whether your food is sweet, salty, bitter or sour. Your sense of smell also helps you to taste things. When you have a cold and cannot smell properly, your food tastes less interesting.

### Find out more about...

light on pages 104 to 105 (Light and sound).

skin and touch on pages 10 to 11 (My outside).

# My outside

Your skin covers every bit of you. It protects the inside of your body in three important ways. It helps to keep out germs, it makes you waterproof, and it stops your body from getting too hot or too cold. Your skin is also full of nerve endings. These send messages to the brain about things you touch, telling it how they feel.

## Fingerprint fun

*Your fingertips have patterns of tiny loops and curves on them. These are your fingerprints. No-one else has fingerprints exactly like yours.
Try painting the tip of your finger and making coloured fingerprints.
You could turn them into fingerprint pictures!*

## Dead on the outside

Did you know that you are dead on the outside? Your skin has two main layers. The outer layer, called the epidermis, is covered in dead cells. But don't worry – there are new cells just underneath. The inner layer is called the dermis. Inside that is a layer of fat, to keep you warm.

## Hot and cold

When you get hot, sweat comes out through holes in your skin, called pores. As the sweat dries on your skin, it takes away heat from your body and cools you down. When you get cold, the pores close up so that the sweat stays in. You may start shivering as well. This warms you by making your muscles produce more heat.

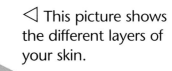

epidermis

dermis

hair

nerve ending

◁ This picture shows the different layers of your skin.

pore

blood vessel

10

## Ouch!

You have cut yourself! Your body must work fast, to stop harmful bacteria getting inside you. Your skin and blood work together to do this. First, blood cells clot together to make a patch over the wound, called a scab. Then special white blood cells kill any bacteria that have got in. Under the scab, new skin cells start to grow.

*Your hair is growing all the time (your nails do this too). If you do not cut your hair, it will normally grow to about a metre in length, then stop. But some people's hair does not stop growing. The longest hair in the world is nearly 4 metres long!*

## Skin colour

What colour is your skin? People's skin can be many different colours, from dark brown to pale pink. It all depends how much melanin (dark colouring) you have in your skin.

 Pale-skinned people have less melanin in their skin. This lets more sunlight into the skin. The sunlight warms the body, which is good when the weather is cold. But it also means that the skin burns more easily.

△ Dark-skinned people have a lot of melanin in their skin. This helps to block out the sun's rays and protect the skin from sunburn.

# Bones and muscles

There is a skeleton inside you. A skeleton is a framework of bones joined together. It holds up your body and gives it shape. There are more than 200 bones in your body, with more than 600 muscles fixed to them! Together the muscles and bones work to move you about.

bone marrow

hard outer bone

softer, living bone

⚠ Bones are hard on the outside, but inside them are softer, living cells. Some big bones, like this thigh bone, have a tube in the middle. The tube is filled with bone marrow, a soft tissue which makes new cells for your blood.

skull

shoulder blade

upper arm

lower arm

ribs

spine

thigh bone

shin bone

heel bone

## Bones

Your skeleton does not just support you. It also protects the soft parts of your body. Your skull is a hard box covering your brain. Your ribs form a cage to guard your heart and lungs.

▽ A muscle works by tightening and then relaxing. This muscle in the upper arm is called the biceps. When it tightens, it pulls up the lower arm. When it relaxes, it lets the lower arm down again.

biceps
tightens

biceps
relaxes

▷ Each muscle is a bundle of thousands of muscle fibres.

## Joints

Joints are the places where your bones meet and join. The bones are held together by strong cords called ligaments. Some joints can move in any direction. Your shoulder and hip joints are like this. Other joints, like the elbows and knees, can only bend in one direction.

## Muscles

A muscle can only do one thing – pull. But all the muscles in your body use their pulling power to do a huge number of jobs. Some only work when you tell them to. These muscles move your body, making it walk or run. Others, such as the muscles that make you breathe, work all the time, even when you are asleep. The most important muscle of all is your heart, which pumps blood around your body.

◁ By using our muscles and bones together, we can make our bodies move in all sorts of amazing ways.

## Busy muscles!

*The muscles that move your eyes are the busiest in the body. They tighten or relax more than 100,000 times every day!*

13

# Lungs and breathing

In…out…in…out. All day and night, we have to go on breathing. When we breathe in, our lungs fill up with air. This contains the oxygen we need to keep us alive. The oxygen goes into our blood. When we breathe out, we push the air out again. Now it contains carbon dioxide, which we want to get rid of.

### Filling the lungs

You have two lungs. Around them, your ribs form a protective cage. Below the lungs is a muscle called the diaphragm.

## Endless blood vessels

*If all the tiny blood vessels in your lungs were laid out in one straight line, they would stretch for nearly 2,400 kilometres! That's all the way from London to Athens, in Greece!*

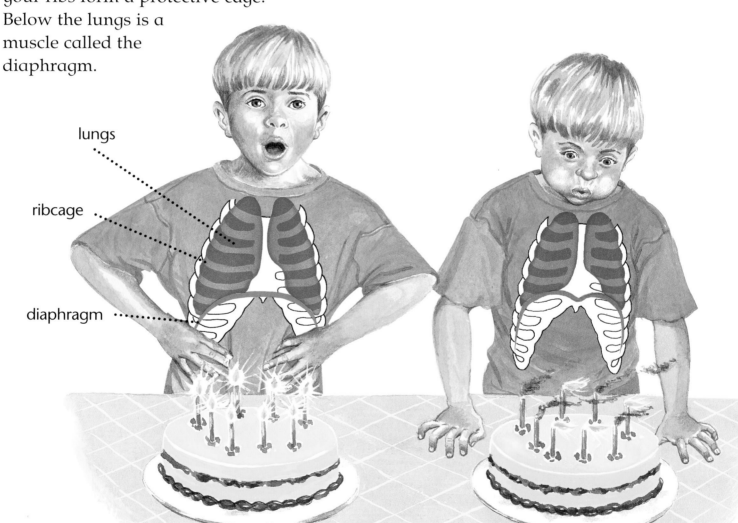

lungs

ribcage

diaphragm

△ When you breathe in, the diaphragm tightens. At the same time, other muscles pull your ribs outwards. This makes your chest and lungs expand, sucking in air through your mouth.

△ To breathe out, the diaphragm and rib muscles relax. Your chest gets smaller again. Your lungs are squashed, and the air in them is squeezed out.

## Inside your lungs

Your lungs are full of tiny air tubes. At the ends of these tubes are little air bags, surrounded by very thin blood vessels. The oxygen from the air passes through the bags and into the blood vessels. At the same time, carbon dioxide passes from the blood vessels into the lungs.

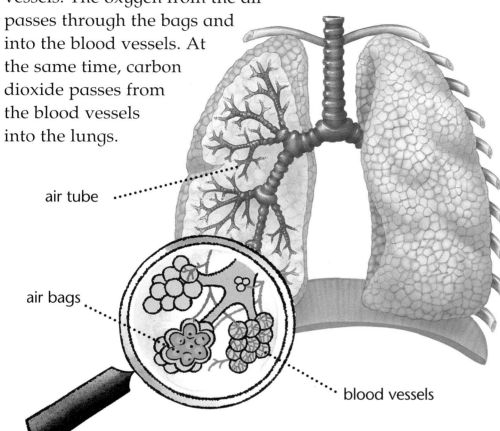

air tube

air bags

blood vessels

△ Some people suffer from an illness called asthma. A muscle tightens in the tubes leading into the lungs. This makes the tubes narrower, and it is hard for the person to breathe. A puff from a special inhaler can make the muscle relax again.

## Breathing fast and slow

When you are asleep, you breathe slowly and gently. Your body is still, so it only needs a small amount of oxygen. When you run about, your body needs more oxygen so you breathe more quickly. Even after you stop running, your body needs to catch up on its oxygen supplies, so you keep panting. Phew!

## Test your lungs

*Find out how much breath you have in your lungs. Fill a bottle with water, and stand it upside down in a bowl of water (make sure the bottle is full). Put one end of a plastic tube, or a bendy drinking straw, into the bottle. Now take one deep breath and blow (gently!) through the tube. Try and empty your lungs. All the air from your lungs will now be trapped in the bottle.*

# Pumping the blood

Blood is your body's transport system. The cells in your body need oxygen to stay alive, and food so that they can grow. Blood carries oxygen and food to all your cells. It also carries carbon dioxide and other waste materials away from the cells, so that your body can get rid of them. Blood is always on the move. Your heart pumps it through a network of tubes called blood vessels. These reach every single part of you.

red cell

white cell

△ Blood is made of cells, which float in a watery liquid called plasma. The red cells carry the oxygen (and give blood its red colour). The white cells help to defend your body against germs.

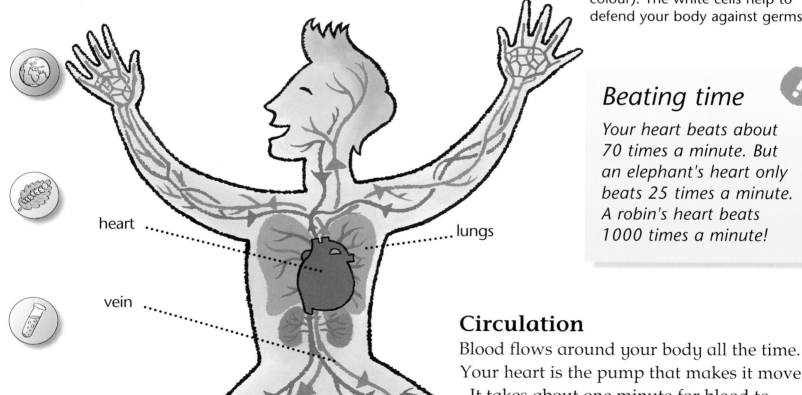

heart

lungs

vein

artery

### Beating time

*Your heart beats about 70 times a minute. But an elephant's heart only beats 25 times a minute. A robin's heart beats 1000 times a minute!*

## Circulation

Blood flows around your body all the time. Your heart is the pump that makes it move. It takes about one minute for blood to travel from your heart to your feet and back again. This is called the circulation of the blood. There are two main kinds of blood vessel – arteries and veins. Arteries carry blood filled with oxygen. Veins carry blood filled with carbon dioxide and other waste materials.

## Heartbeats

Your heart is a muscle about as big as your fist.
Inside, there are four main parts, or chambers.
Each one is a separate pump. The heart muscle
tightens and relaxes about 70 times every minute.
At each "beat" it pushes blood through
the heart, and out to the
lungs and the body.

blood taking waste to the lungs

blood taking oxygen to the body

blood bringing waste from the body

blood bringing oxygen from the lungs

▷ Doctors use a
special instrument to
test your blood
pressure. This tells
them how strongly
blood is being pumped
through your blood
vessels. Very low or
very high blood
pressure can be a sign
that you are unwell.

*Find out more about . . .*

how exercise helps
keep your heart strong
on pages 28 to 29
(A healthy life).

# My brain and nerves

Inside your head is your brain. This is the control centre of your body. Your brain does your thinking and remembering, and sends out orders to the body about speaking, moving and feeling. It is connected to the rest of your body by cords called nerves. The nerves carry messages between the brain and the body.

▷ Your brain looks grey and wrinkled, like a giant walnut. It has several different parts, each with its own job to do. Each of your five senses has its own area of the brain.

## A bundle of nerves

Messages from your brain go into your spinal cord. This is a bundle of nerves running down the middle of your back. Smaller nerves branch off from the spinal cord to every part of your body. The whole network is called your nervous system.

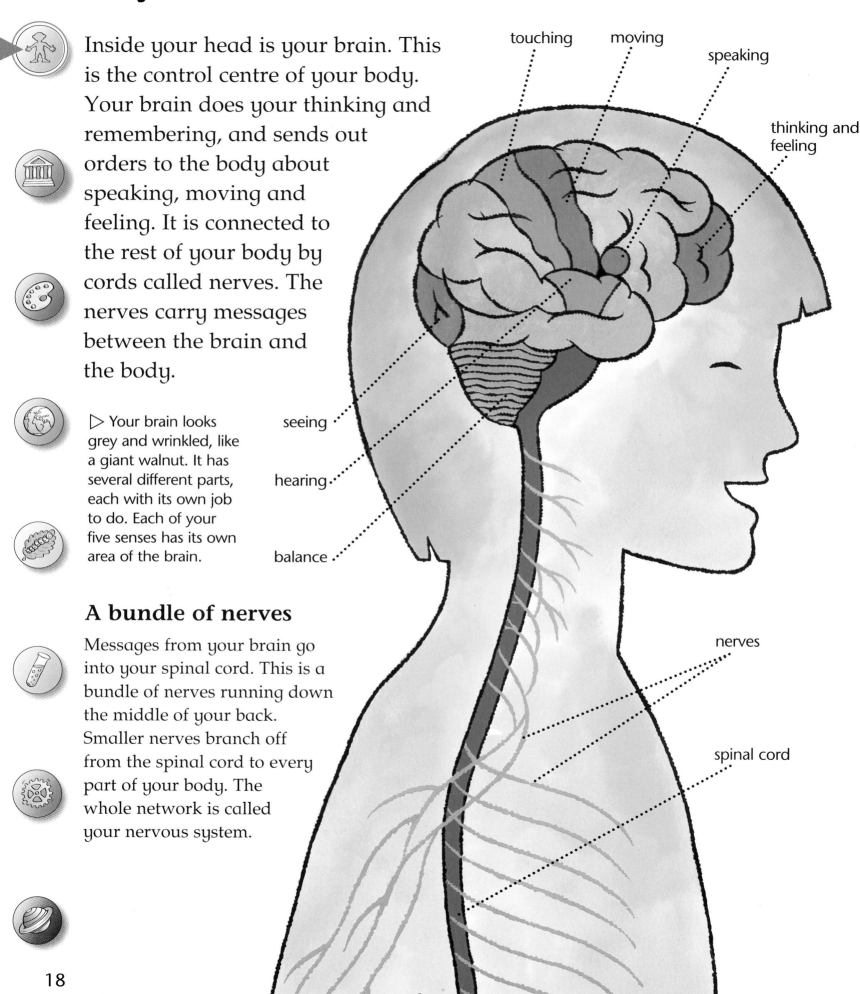

touching
moving
speaking
thinking and feeling
seeing
hearing
balance
nerves
spinal cord

## Test your memory

*This card game is a good test of your memory.*

*Lay out all the cards in the pack on a table or the floor, face down. Make sure you don't see any of the cards as you put them down. Whoever is going first turns over two cards. If they have the same number, he or she can pick them up, and have another go. If they are different, they must turn them face down again. Now it is the next person's turn . . .*

*The winner is the one with the most pairs when all the cards have been picked up.*

## The brain in action

Your brain is always busy, getting messages then sending its own messages out. Here's how the brain goes into action when you meet someone you know.

1. You see someone walking towards you. Your eyes send a picture of the person to your brain.

2. Your brain recognizes the picture. It is your friend Alfie! You want to say hello. Your brain sends a message to your arm, and another to your mouth.

3. Your arm obeys the order, and starts to wave. Your mouth shouts out "Hello, Alfie!".

## ! Quick thinking

*Messages whizz to and from the brain at speeds of up to 290 kilometres per hour. That's faster than the fastest express train!*

# What happens to food?

Like a car, your body needs fuel to keep it going. A car runs on petrol: you keep going with food. The food gives you energy and helps you to grow. But first your body has to break down the food into its different parts. Some parts are useful to the body, others are waste. This process is called digestion.

## A tube through your body

Food travels through your body along a long tube called the gut. The journey may take over a day. Your gut is coiled up inside your body, and is more than six metres long. It is made up of several different parts, each with its own job to do.

Food goes into your body through the mouth. Your teeth break it up, then your tongue pushes it to the back of your mouth. Gulp!

Muscles in your gullet squeeze the food straight down into the stomach.

The stomach muscles churn up the food with special liquids, which help to break the food down.

▽ Your teeth are good at grinding up your food before it goes to your gut. But sugar and other food and drink can damage the hard enamel on the outside. Your teeth can get holes. If a hole reaches the nerve, you will get toothache. So keep your teeth clean!

hole    enamel

nerve ···

## Liver and kidneys

Your liver is one of the busiest parts of your body. It has nearly 500 different jobs to do! Blood comes to the liver from your intestines, carrying useful materials from your food. The liver takes the goodness out of the food and sends it on for other parts of the body to use.

Your kidneys help to keep your blood clean. As blood passes through them, they take out unwanted material and turn it into a liquid called urine. Urine is wee. It is stored in your bladder until you go to the toilet.

........ liver

........ kidney

........ bladder

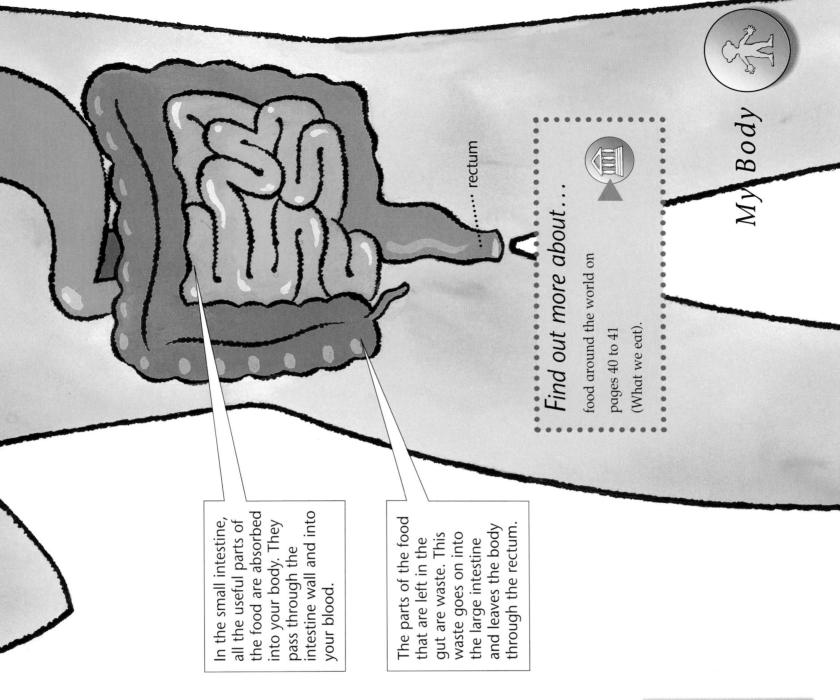

rectum

In the small intestine, all the useful parts of the food are absorbed into your body. They pass through the intestine wall and into your blood.

The parts of the food that are left in the gut are waste. This waste goes on into the large intestine and leaves the body through the rectum.

*Find out more about…*

food around the world on pages 40 to 41 (What we eat).

**!** *A food mountain*

*During your lifetime, you will eat about 50 tonnes of food, and drink about 50,000 litres of liquid.*

*My Body*

21

# Being born

This is the story of how a baby grows. It takes two people to make a baby – a mother and a father. Inside the mother is an egg, smaller than a full stop. Inside the father are lots of sperms, even tinier than the egg. The story begins when the sperms travel from the father's body into the mother's body.

## Speedy opossums

*Humans take about 9 months to be born. Some other animals take much longer. A baby elephant grows for about 20 months before it is born. The fastest-growing animal baby of all is the opossum – it takes as little as 8 days to be born!*

◁ This picture has been magnified many times. It shows a sperm joining up with an egg. The sperm looks a bit like a tadpole.

 sperm

 egg

umbilical cord

this is the baby's real size ....

## The baby begins

The sperms travel through the mother's body until they reach the egg. Then one sperm joins with the egg, and together they make the first cell of the new baby.  The baby starts to grow in a part of the mother's body called the "uterus". The egg splits to make two cells . . . then four . . . then eight, and so on.

uterus

△ This baby is about six weeks old. It is no longer just a ball of cells, but it is very small. The baby gets food from its mother, through a special tube called the umbilical cord.

▽ After just three months, the baby is fully formed. It has arms and legs, fingers and toes, as well as eyes, ears, nose and a mouth. But it is still very tiny. (The purple shape shows the baby's real size.)

▽ After seven months the baby has grown much bigger (the purple shape shows its real size). Babies in the uterus sleep and wake, just like us. Some scientists even think that they have dreams. The baby grows for two more months, until it is nine months old. Then it is born.

Find out more about...

how we change
as we get older
on pages 24 to 25
(Growing up).

▷ This baby has just been born. The muscles in the mother's uterus have pushed the baby out into the world. It does not need its umbilical cord any more, so the doctor cuts it. The newborn baby feeds on milk from its mother's breasts.

# Growing up

From the moment you are born, you grow very quickly. You go on growing all through childhood. But it is not just your body that changes. You find out about the world around you, and about how to do things. You learn how to get on with other people. You go on changing all through your life, learning new skills and having new experiences.

◁ Babies learn quickly. Soon they can smile and laugh, grip with their hands, roll over and make all sorts of noises. By the age of two, they can walk and talk.

▷ By the age of eight, children can use their bodies to run, dance and play games. Their world has become much bigger. They go to school, and have friends to share jokes and secrets.

## Shrinking every day

*Every day, you shrink by about 8 millimetres! As you stand or sit, your weight pushes down on your spine and makes you shorter. But at night, when you lie down, your spine relaxes and stretches out again.*

△ From about ten, boys and girls slowly begin to turn into adults. Girls become more rounded, and their breasts start to grow. Boys grow more hair on their bodies, and their voices get deeper. Soon, boys and girls become interested in going out together.

▽ By about twenty, children have changed into adults. Their bodies are fully developed, and they stop growing taller. Now they are ready to have babies of their own.

△ As people get older, their bodies often slow down. Many people stop working and have more leisure time. Their own children have grown up, but they may have grandchildren, or even great-grandchildren who come to visit them.

## Living longer

Today we grow more food and have better medicines than in the past, so people live longer. A hundred years ago, people in the USA lived on average to the age of 47. Today, someone living in the USA can expect to live to 75 or more.

## Find out more about...

children in other countries on pages 44 to 47 (Children of the world).

your relations on page 30 (Families).

# Illness

You feel hot. You shiver. Your head aches. What is happening? You are ill! Your body is under attack from tiny germs. There are many sorts of germs, and they cause many different illnesses. Some, such as chickenpox or a cold, are not very serious. But others can be dangerous.

◁ The germ in this picture is called a bacterium. It has been magnified many times.

## Getting ill

You can catch an illness from someone else if germs from them get into your body. Germs carry some diseases from one person to another. These are called infectious diseases. The germs travel through the air, or live in food, or get passed on when people cough or sneeze.

▷ Your body can fight off some illnesses by itself. The best way to cure a bad cold or flu is to stay at home and rest in bed.

## At the doctor's

Sometimes when you are ill, you need to go to see the doctor. Doctors often listen to your chest with a special instrument called a stethoscope. They may also give you medicines or pills, to help fight off germs.

△ All through history, scientists have invented new medicines, new machines and new ways to fight against disease. One important invention is the X-ray machine, which can take pictures of the insides of our bodies. This photograph shows an early X-ray machine.

## Hospitals

If you are very ill you will have to go to hospital. You may have a serious disease, or have had a bad accident. At the hospital, doctors and nurses give you special care. If something has gone wrong inside your body, you may need an operation. You are taken to a special room called an operating theatre, where you are put to sleep for a short time. Then the doctor can operate on you.

### Find out more about . . .

health and fitness on page 28 (A healthy life).

food to keep you healthy on pages 40 to 41 (What we eat).

# A healthy life

You can fight against many kinds of illness – before they even start! Disease has less of a chance if you keep your body fit and healthy. Here are three important ways to do that:

## Keep clean

Keeping your body clean helps get rid of germs. If these germs got into your body, they could make you ill. Always wash your hands after using the toilet, and before you touch any food.

## Keep moving

Your body likes to be given work to do. Walking, running, swimming and cycling are all good kinds of exercise. Exercise keeps your heart and other muscles in shape, and your bones strong. It gets your blood flowing quickly through your body. All these things make your body healthier.

## Eat well

Everyone knows that too many fatty or sugary foods are bad for you. But it is not good to eat too much of any one kind of food. Make sure that your meals contain a mixture of good things: carbohydrate foods such as bread and pasta, fatty foods such as milk and cheese, and high-protein foods such as meat and fish.

△ This food pyramid is a guide to healthy eating. At the bottom are the foods you should eat most of. Only eat a little of the foods right at the top.

# People and Places

You live on the Earth, together with millions of other people. Some people live in villages, some in crowded cities, some on wide plains, some in forests and some in the mountains. But all of us need the same basic things – food, shelter, a family and friends. We find these things in many different ways.

# Families

Do you live on your own? Or are you part of a family? A family is a group of people who are related to each other. They care for each other, and share money, food and housework. You are most closely related to your parents, brothers and sisters. But you have many other relatives.

## My great-grandparents' generation

great-grandfather   great-grandmother    great-grandfather   great-grandmother    great-grandfather   great-grandmother    great-grandfather   great-grandmother

## My grandparents' generation

great uncle    great aunt    grandfather    grandmother    grandfather    grandmother    great uncle    great aunt

## My parents' generation

uncle    aunt     father    mother     uncle    aunt

This is called a family "tree". Actually, it looks more like a net or a web. It shows how members of a family are related to each other. The tree is divided into different "generations". In each generation, the people are about the same age.

## My generation

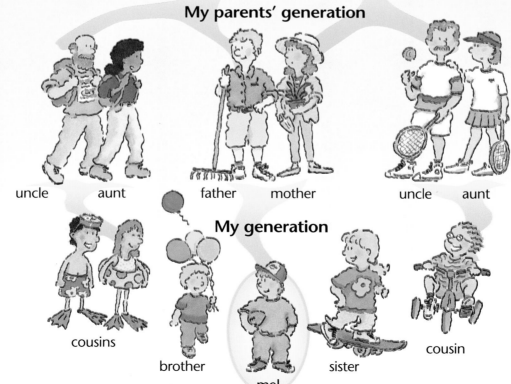

cousins

brother

me!

sister

cousin

30

## Different families

You may live in a small family – just you and one or two parents, perhaps brothers and sisters too. But not all family groups are the same. In some families only one parent lives with the children. Other families are much bigger, with children, parents, grandparents, aunts, uncles and cousins all living together in an extended family.

### Babies every second!

*There are more than 5,800 million people in the world. And every day about 400,000 more babies are born. That's 255 every minute!*

◁ Many families live together in this big house in Borneo. Up to fifty families may have their home in one "longhouse".

## Family likeness

People often look similar to their brothers or sisters, or to their mother or father. We inherit the way we look from our parents. Can you guess the connection between these three children? They are a girl, her mother, and her grandmother. Each of them was photographed when she was about three years old.

### Find out about your family

*Find out about your own family tree. Ask older people in your family to help you. See how far back in time you can go. Where do your grandparents come from? What about your great-grandparents? When were they born? What jobs did they do?*

# Where we live

We all have a place to live in, which we call home. Your home has a roof and walls to protect you from the weather. It is the place where you eat and go to sleep, where you and your family can be together.

Our homes come in all shapes and sizes, from tall apartment buildings in cities to small shelters made by people in hot countries to shade them from the sun. Houses such as caravans and tents can even move from place to place.

## What are houses made of?

People build their houses out of many different materials. Some houses are built with materials that can easily be found nearby, such as wood, stone or clay. Other houses may be built from materials such as concrete, steel and glass, which may be made in faraway factories.

△ A giant block of flats in Bombay, India, built of modern materials. The frame inside is made of steel girders, the walls and floors are concrete. There are lots of large glass windows.

△ This house in southern Africa is made of clay. Clay is good for building houses – as long as there isn't too much rain! In wetter countries, the clay is baked into bricks to make it waterproof

△ A stone house in Edinburgh, Scotland. This house was built from blocks of stone cut out of the local rocks. The roof is made of slate, another kind of stone.

◁ In big cities like Tokyo in Japan, thousands of people live and work close together. Cities are busy and noisy, but they have plenty of shops, hospitals, buses and other useful services.

## Villages, towns and cities

Our homes are usually grouped together. A few people, like farmers, live in houses which are built on their own, in the middle of large areas of land. A village is a small group of homes in a rural area. Some villages grow into towns, and some towns into big cities. Where would you rather live – in a city, a town, or in the countryside?

## Underground cities

*In crowded cities, people build skyscrapers upwards. But in Japan, builders are now thinking of going downwards. They are planning cities under the ground, where over 100,000 people will live and work. Sunlight for these underground cities will be reflected down from the surface by mirrors!*

△ This Mongolian tent is called a yurt. The family need a home that is easy to move, because they travel from place to place with their herds of animals. The covering is of thick felt, fitted over a wooden frame.

△ This log house in Russia is made of wood, cut from the forests all around. There is plenty of firewood to keep the house warm through the long, cold winters.

## Find out more about...

different materials on pages 102 to 103 (Building blocks)

tall buildings on pages 118 to 119 (Strong structures)

# Life in a town

A town is like a huge, complicated machine. It has thousands of different parts, which all have to work together to make it run smoothly. There are the buildings – shops, offices, houses and factories. Between the buildings are roads for cars, lorries, bicycles and buses. But the most important parts of all are the people who live and work in the town.

34

## Keeping a town running

A town needs more than just roads and buildings to keep it going. Food has to be brought in by truck or train, and water comes in pipes from big lakes called reservoirs. As the town gets bigger, people need buses and trains to get around. The town needs rubbish collectors, and sewage pipes to get rid of dirty water. It also needs people to keep everything running.

## What can you find?

Look at this busy town. It has grown from a small old town to a large new one. See if you can spot all the things in the list below. Some of them are easy to find – others are harder!

the railway station

the market place, with its stalls

the park, with its playground

a school

a supermarket

boating on the river

the police station

an old church

the cinema

the hospital

the sports centre

flats on the edge of town

a building site

the business park, with its factories and workshops

## Find out more about...

the different kinds of places people live on pages 44 to 47 (Children of the World).

# People at work

Most of us have to work. You work at school. Grown-ups work at thousands of different kinds of jobs. They do this so that they can provide food and clothes for their families and look after them. Some people grow their own food or make their clothes. Others are paid money for their work. With this money they can buy food, clothes and other things they need.

▽ The Masai people of East Africa are very proud of their cattle. They rarely eat them for meat. Instead they drink the animals' milk and blood.

▽ These fishermen from Japan catch fish in huge nets. Their boat is called a trawler.

## Hunters and gatherers

The simplest way to get food is to catch it yourself. For thousands of years, people have gathered fruit and vegetables, and hunted animals. If they do not find anything, they go hungry! Today, there are still hunters and gatherers in a few parts of the world. And there are many other people, like fishermen, who catch food to sell.

## Growers and herders

Farmers and herders use the land to grow food. Farmers plough the land and sow crops, such as wheat and rice. Or they look after animals – cattle, pigs, sheep, goats and chickens. Herders travel with their animals. If there is not enough grass for the herd, they move on. From the animals they get meat and other important foods, such as milk and wool.

## Makers

Some people work at making things for others to buy. Craft workers use their hands and simple tools to make beautiful objects such as clay pots or woollen rugs. In factories, people use machines to make all sorts of goods, from cars to toothbrushes.

△ To make patterned rugs, these Indian women must first spin the wool on a spinning wheel, then dye it different colours. They then weave the different colours together on a loom.

# People and Places

## People who help us

Many workers do not make or grow anything. They may work in offices, banks or libraries. They may sell things in shops. Or they may help other people. Nurses and doctors look after us when we are sick. Bus and train drivers take us from place to place. Police officers and firefighters help to protect us and our property.

△ Firefighters wear special protective clothes for fighting fires. They carry air tanks and breathing masks, so that they do not choke on the smoke inside burning buildings.

*Find out more about . . .*

what people do in other countries

on pages 44 to 47 (Children of the world).

# People at play

School's over! Work's finished! What are you going to do in your free time? Two hundred years ago, people had little time for fun. They worked long hours, and only had one day off a week. This still happens in many parts of the world today. But now machines do a lot of our work for us. We have more free time than before – and many more ways of enjoying it.

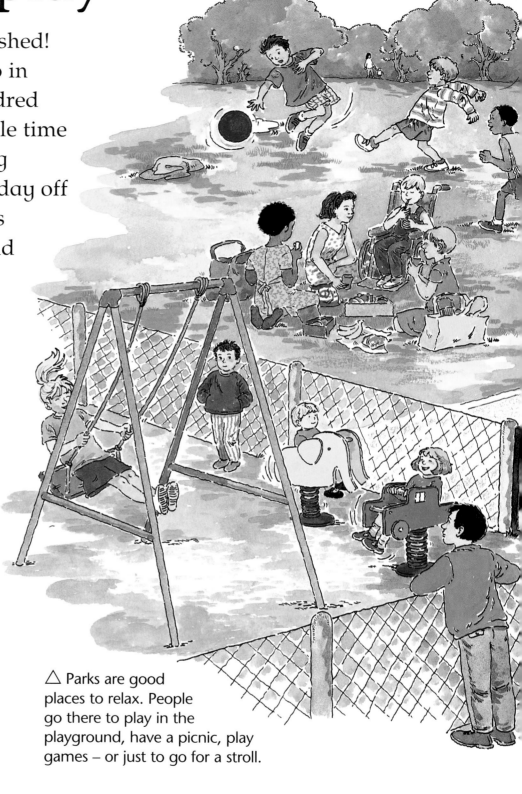

△ Parks are good places to relax. People go there to play in the playground, have a picnic, play games – or just to go for a stroll.

## Relaxing

Many people like to relax in their free time. They might take it easy at home, chatting with friends or reading. They might also go out, to the park or to the cinema. But the most popular way of relaxing is to watch television.

## Playing sport

There are hundreds of different sports and games to choose from. Some can be played almost anywhere. You can play football in the park, or in your garden. You can play baseball on a beach. But other sports, like skiing or swimming, need special settings or equipment.

◁ Football is a very old game. A kind of football was probably played in China over 2,000 years ago. Soccer is the most popular football game in the world.

△ Basketball is a game for two teams of players. To score points you have to throw the ball into your opponent's basketball net.

## Going on holiday

Every year, millions of people go away on holiday. They may go to the seaside or countryside in their own country, or they may go abroad. Modern aircraft can take us far from home very quickly. It is possible to fly 5,500 kilometres from New York to Paris in about seven hours!

## Playground games

*Children have always made up their own games to play. Some, like hide-and-seek, are played all over the world. But others are less well-known. Here are two for you to try.*

**Ear and nose** (from Iran)
Stand in a circle. One person pulls the ear, or nose, or hair of the person to the left (gently!). They do the same to the person on their left – and so on, round the circle. Then the first player starts again, and pulls a different part of the body. You must not laugh. If you do, you are out.

**"Keep the cattle in"** (from Botswana)
All the players except two hold hands in a ring and move slowly round. The two players inside the ring are the "cattle". As the ring moves round, the cattle try to run out under people's arms. If they get out, they join the ring, and the ones who let them escape become the cattle.

# What we eat

We all have to eat to stay alive. Good food gives us energy and keeps our bodies healthy. It is also fun to cook and eat. Around the world, people have learned to prepare the food they grow or buy in many different ways. But in all parts of the world, a healthy meal has the same types of food in it.

## A healthy meal

The biggest part of a healthy meal is something filling, like rice, bread or potatoes. This is called a "staple" food. With this staple food we eat vegetables or fruit, and a food with plenty of protein, such as meat, fish or beans. "Dairy products" – things like milk and cheese – are also good protein foods.

◁ This picture shows some of the foods we need for a healthy diet. Can you work out which are staple foods?

# Favourite foods in . . .

People in different parts of the world eat very different meals! Here are some examples from around the world.

### Italy
Pizza. The base is made from bread dough. This is covered with cheese, tomatoes and many other toppings. The bread dough is made from wheat.

### The USA
Beefburgers, chips and beans. The beef comes from cattle. The potatoes for the chips come from plants grown in the fields. The beans are from plants, too.

### Africa
Groundnut stew with fufu. The stew is chicken cooked in a groundnut (peanut) sauce. Fufu are dumplings made from vegetables such as cassava, yams or potatoes.

### Japan
Japanese people eat a lot of fish, and it is often served raw. Sashimi is raw fish, radish and seaweed, served with soy sauce and raw vegetables carved in the shapes of flowers.

## Faraway foods

*Some of the food you buy may have travelled a long way to get to the shops. Here's how to find out where your food has come from. Go to your store cupboard or fridge, and look at the tins and packets inside. Read the labels carefully. Somewhere it will tell you where the food was grown or packed. For instance, a pack of butter may say "Produce of New Zealand". A tin of tomatoes may say "Produce of Italy". If there's a country you do not know, look it up on a world map.*

## Find out more about . . .

what happens to food when you eat it, on pages 20 to 21 (What happens to food).

healthy eating on page 28 (A healthy life).

# What we believe

Most people have a religion. This means that they believe in a power outside their ordinary lives. They often have a name for this power – a God or gods. There are hundreds of different religions in the world. Each religion has its own way of worshipping its God or gods, and a special set of rules for its believers.

▷ Hannukah is the Jewish festival of lights. To celebrate, people light candles on a special Hannukah candlestick.

## Judaism

Judaism is the religion of the Jews. Like the Christians and Muslims, they believe that there is one God, who made the world. The homeland of the Jews is Israel in the Middle East, but Jews now live in many parts of the world. Saturday is the Jewish day of prayer, when Jews rest from work. They go to a service in a synagogue, their place of worship. They read from the Torah and the Book of Prophets, their holy books.

## Christianity

Christians follow the teachings of Jesus Christ. They believe he was God's son who came to live on Earth, where he was put to death on a cross, and then came to life again. There are many different Christian groups. One of the biggest is the Roman Catholic Church. Sunday is the holy day for Christians. They go to a church to worship God and Jesus Christ.

▷ Christians celebrate the birth of Jesus at Christmas by singing carols.

# People and Places

▽ Ramadan is the Muslim special month of fasting. At the end of the month, they celebrate!

## Islam

People who follow the Islamic religion are Muslims. They believe that there is one God, called Allah. They follow the teachings of the Prophet Mohammed, who lived in Arabia long ago. Muslims must follow five strict rules. They must believe in Allah, pray five times each day, give money to the poor, travel at least once to the holy city of Mecca, and fast (eat no daytime food) for one month each year.

## Hinduism

Hindus worship many gods. Among the most important are Brahma, who made the world, Vishnu, who preserves life, and Shiva, who destroys life. Hindus believe that, after we die, we are born again in a new form. Hinduism is the main religion of India, and other countries such as Sri Lanka and Indonesia. Many Hindus have special places in their homes called shrines, decorated with statues or pictures of their favourite gods.

△ Diwali is the Hindu festival of lights, at their New Year. Children make special patterns with coloured sand, called Rangoli patterns.

▽ Wesak is the most important Buddhist festival. People decorate their houses and the streets with lanterns and candles.

## Buddhism

Buddhists have no gods. They believe that unhappiness and pain are caused by human greediness. Buddhists find happiness by living a simple life. They follow the teachings of an Indian prince, who became known as the Buddha. Each day, they spend time meditating. They sit still and quiet and relax their minds, to forget the selfishness of everyday life.

43

# Children of the world

What would it be like to live in another country? Many parts of your life would be very different – your home, your school, your games, your holidays. Here are children from around the world to tell you about their lives.

My name is Natasha. I live in a city in Russia. My home is a tiny flat. We have to share the kitchen and bathroom with our neighbours. Winters are very cold, and I wear a fur hat and coat to school. On summer weekends we all go to our other home in the countryside. There, we can climb trees and hunt for mushrooms.

My name is Moktar. I live in the desert in Mali. My family does not stay in one place. We have to get food for our goats and camels – and food is hard to find here. So we are often on the move. My home is a tent, and I wear a white cloth round my head to protect me from the burning sun.

My name is Kathleen. I live in a village in Ireland. The nearest town is over 15 kilometres away. We have a small house with a big garden, where we keep two goats and some hens. In summer, I like to play outside with my pet kitten Jess. But in winter, I sit in front of a cosy fire and watch television.

My name is Fatima. I live in a city in Turkey. My mother plaits my long hair every morning, ready for school. Lessons finish at lunchtime. In the afternoon, my mother sends me to buy fruit and vegetables at the market. I take care to choose only the best and cheapest. As a reward, I buy a snack of baked lamb wrapped in bread.

My name is Mariam. I live in a village in Tanzania. Before I go to school, I have work to do. I fetch water from the well, then drive my family's nine cows out into the fields. But when school is over, there is plenty of time for fun. I play football, or make wooden toys for my little brothers and sisters.

My name is Isaac. I live on a kibbutz, or farm community, in Israel. Many other families live there too. Every day I go to school at a children's house, while my parents are at work. When lessons are over, I help in the garden and feed the animals at our zoo. At weekends, I like to go fishing at the seaside.

My name is Sanjay. I live in a village in India. My family is very poor, so my brothers all go out to work. But I am lucky – I go to school. I get up early each morning and walk to the school. When it gets very hot, we have lessons outside in the shade of a tree.

My name is Inga. I live in a small town in Sweden. The land is very flat here, so I like to go out on my bicycle. When it is snowy, I ski to school. We start lessons very early – at 8 o'clock! Once a week I have dancing lessons. I am also learning to play the violin.

My name is David. I live in a small town in Australia. We are a long way from the nearest big city. All the same, there is plenty to do here. I go swimming and surfing in the sea – but not when there are jellyfish around! I also like to play rugby and go fishing. The weather is always warm, and I wear shorts all year round.

My name is Mario. I live in a city in El Salvador. This is a very poor country. Our house is made of wood and metal sheets, and we have no bathroom. In the mornings, I work in a carpenter's shop. In the afternoon I go to school. After that, I feel very tired, but I still find time to fly my kite, or practise on my guitar.

My name is Lin. My home is a city in China. I have to go to school every day except Sunday. When I get there, I help to clean the classrooms and the yard. Then we all do special exercises before classes begin. On Sundays, I like to go to the park and play ping-pong (table tennis).

My name is Hina. My home is a Polynesian island in the Pacific Ocean. The weather is hot all year round, so we do nearly everything out of doors. I like to go swimming and fishing in the warm sea around the island. Many tourists come here. I help my mother to sell them hand-made baskets and mats from her stall.

My name is Greg. I live outside a small town in the USA. My brother and I have a long walk to catch the bus that takes us to school in the town. In winter, when thick snow covers the ground, the walk takes even longer. That is because we have snowball fights! In summer, Mum and Dad take us camping in the mountains, where there are no roads or people.

My name is Zulecha. I live in a city in Malaysia. My family are Muslim, so I usually wear traditional Muslim clothes, including a white head-dress. When school is over, I help my mother with the cooking and cleaning. We go to prayers every Friday at the special women-only mosque near our home. The men go to their own mosque.

My name is Roberto. I live on a farm in Argentina. My father works for the farm owner, and helps look after his huge herd of cattle. Like most people in Argentina, we eat a lot of meat. At the end of the day, we often have a barbecue. I like to ride my pony around the big farm. I am learning to play polo, which is an exciting horseback game with sticks and a ball.

## A special letter

*What are the special things in your life? Write a letter to one of these children, telling them about what you do every day – your home, your school and the things you like doing best.*

My name is Lucky. My home is a village in Greenland. It is very cold all the time. In winter, it is dark all day and even the sea freezes over! Our little wooden house is kept warm by a coal stove, and I have to wear thick fur clothes. When I grow up, I want to be a hunter like my father.

# How we used to live

People have been on Earth for a very long time. Over thousands of years, we have found ways of growing more food on it. We have built great towns and cities. And we have invented amazing machines and medicines, which have made life safer and more comfortable.

▷ 100,000 years ago in Africa, people lived in small bands. They hunted wild animals and gathered plants to eat, and cooked them on wood fires. They used animal skins to make clothes, or to cover a rough shelter made of tree branches.

▷ 4,000 years ago, in Egypt, people could grow enough food to last them all year. They had time left over for other things – pottery, metalwork, and building the first cities. They also built massive pyramids, where Egypt's kings, or pharaohs, were buried.

△ 500 years ago in Peru, the Inca people built up a huge and very rich empire. This was a land of tall mountains and deep valleys. The Incas built a network of roads and suspension bridges across the mountains. Along these went fast runners, carrying messages, and slower pack animals, carrying goods.

△ 10,000 years ago, in the Middle East, people first learned to be farmers. They grew food grains such as wheat and barley, and made them into bread and flour. People also kept herds of sheep or goats. Now they could have bread, milk and meat whenever they wanted!

◁ 2,000 years ago Rome, in Italy, was the strongest city in the world. Roman armies had conquered an empire stretching from Britain to Egypt. The Romans were great builders. They built huge buildings, roads, bridges and walls. You can still see some of them today.

◁ 1,000 years ago, China was already a huge and crowded country. And the Chinese had invented many important things long before the rest of the world knew about them. Chinese people were already printing on paper, telling the time with clocks, farming their fields with iron ploughs, and using gunpowder in bombs and fireworks.

◁ 100 years ago, North America began to fill up with people. Millions of settlers came from poor parts of Europe, hoping to find a new life. They landed on the east coast of the USA. Many travelled westwards across rivers, plains and mountains. They started farms, grew corn and raised herds of cattle. They built small towns, which grew into cities.

## Find out more about...

artists through history on
pages 54 to 55
(Painting and sculpture).

# Exploring the world

A thousand years ago, huge areas of the world had never been explored. Some people thought that the Earth was flat – if a ship sailed too far, it might fall off the edge! But since then travellers have been brave enough to explore this unknown world.

▷ Ibn Battuta lived about 600 years ago He spent most of his life exploring. From his home in North Africa, he went to Arabia, India and as far as China. He even crossed the Sahara Desert.

◁ About 500 years ago, Vasco da Gama sailed from Europe right round the tip of Africa. He went all the way to India.

▷ In 1492 Christopher Columbus sailed westwards from Spain across the Atlantic Ocean. He wanted to reach China and Japan, but he found America in the way! No Europeans knew it was there.

◁ Ferdinand Magellan found a channel which took him into the vast Pacific Ocean. In 1522 one of his ships became the first to sail right round the world. This proved that the world was round, not flat.

▷ In 1911 Roald Amundsen became the first person to reach the South Pole. He used husky dogs to pull the heavy sledges full of supplies. Later, he went to the North Pole as well – by balloon.

# The Arts

Do you paint or draw? Do you make things out of modelling clay, or cardboard? Do you sing, or dance, or play an instrument? Perhaps you make up stories and write them down, or perform plays with your friends. Painting, drawing, music, dance, stories and plays are all arts. People use arts in all kinds of ways – to tell stories, to express feelings, to make beautiful things – and for fun!

# Music and dance

Music is a set of sounds – but not just any sounds. They need to please or excite us. The sounds are usually arranged to make a tune. Different sounds can also be played together to make harmonies. Music needs a regular beat, or rhythm, and rhythm is a vital part of dancing. This is why music and dance so often go together.

## Making music

You can make music in all sorts of ways. You can sing with your voice, either on your own, or with other people. You can hit an instrument, such as a drum or a gong. You can blow into an instrument such as a saxophone or a whistle. You can pluck the strings of an instrument such as a guitar. Each part of the world has its own kind of music, and its own instruments to play it on.

## Dancing about

Do you jump up and down when you are excited? That is a kind of dancing! In most dances, people move their bodies in time to music or a rhythm. At parties and special celebrations, people dance together to enjoy themselves. But there are other kinds of dancing, which are performed for people to watch. The dancers often wear costumes, and train for many years to learn the skills they need.

## *Make your own music*

*You can have your very own orchestra with these simple instruments.*

*Scratcher: wrap sandpaper round two small blocks of wood. Then rub the blocks together in a regular rhythm.*

*Kazoo: wrap a piece of greaseproof paper round a comb. Press the comb against your mouth and hum.*

*Musical straws: flatten one end of a straw, and snip it to a point. Blow hard down the straw to make a sound. Straws of different lengths will make different notes.*

### Find out more about . . .

sound on pages 110 to 111 (Light and sound).

# Painting and sculpture

We like to make pictures. Some show what we see around us. Others are pictures of imaginary things. Over thousands of years, we have learned many ways of making these pictures. We can put paint marks on paper, or canvas – or even walls. We can carve figures out of wood or stone. We can make shapes with metal or clay.

△ Many Christian churches have windows made of stained, or coloured, glass. The pictures on them often tell stories from the Bible.

# What are pictures for?

Paintings and sculptures can have lots of uses. They can tell stories, about anything from great adventures to everyday events. They can show gods or saints and can be used as holy objects. They can show what famous people looked like.
But, most of all, pictures are something to enjoy!

▷ This gold mask shows the face of a king who died in Greece over 3,500 years ago.

△ Many mosques (Muslim places of prayer) have tiled patterns all over the walls and ceilings. The patterns are beautiful combinations of shapes and colours.

△ This picture is a copy of a painting by an Italian artist. It shows a scene from the story of Saint George and the dragon. Saint George was a knight who fought and killed a fierce dragon to stop it from eating the king's daughter.

△ The children in this picture are using all kinds of materials to make pictures and models. How many different kinds of material can you see?

◁ These hand prints were done for fun. The bright colours and bold shapes look happy and full of energy.

# Telling stories

Everybody likes a story. Even before people had learned to write, they told stories to each other out loud. Today, we have many ways of telling stories. In a play or a film, the actors use movement and speech. They pretend to be the people in the tale. In a book, the author uses written words to tell us what happens.

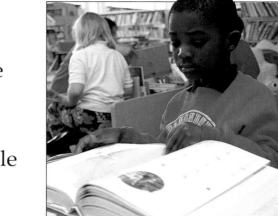

## Acting out stories

People first performed plays in Greece, over 2,500 years ago. A Greek theatre had no roof, and the audience sat on stone seats. Since then, many different kinds of plays (or drama) have grown up, in different parts of the world.

▽ In this shadow play, there are puppets instead of actors. A light behind the flat puppets throws their shadows onto a screen.

△ A theatre in ancient Greece. The ruins of many old theatres can still be seen today.

## Stories in books

The easiest place to find a good story is in your local library. Most towns have their own library, packed with thousands of books. Some stories will be very old, and were first written down many centuries ago. Others will be brand new, for new stories are being written all the time.

△ A modern theatre with a raised stage, powerful lights and realistic scenery.

## Stories on film

On a film, you can see the actors. What you cannot see are the dozens of other people who help to make the film. Some people film the action with the camera, or record the words and sounds. Some people work the powerful lights which make each scene look clear. Some people make the scenery, or special effects such as rain or snow. Most important of all is the director, who is in charge of everyone else.

## Make a flip book

*You can make your own moving pictures! Take a sheet of A4 paper, and ask an adult to help you cut it into 16 equal pieces. Draw a picture of a figure on the first piece. Now carefully copy that figure on to the second piece, but with a small difference: perhaps the arms have moved a little. Draw a figure on each of the other pieces, each time changing it a little. Now staple your pieces together in order, and try quickly flipping through the pages. Your figure will seem to move!*

◁ Action films often have scenes where the actors have to do difficult and dangerous tricks. These scenes are often done by special actors called "stunt people". In this picture, the stunt man is dropping from an aeroplane on to a moving truck.

# Using words

We use words every day. We say "Hello" or "Thank you". We ask people for things. We tell them news about what is happening, or how we feel. But we can also put all these words down on paper, using one of our greatest inventions: writing.

## How did writing begin?

Long ago, there was no way of keeping records or setting down stories. People had to remember everything. Then, about 5,000 years ago, people in the Middle East began to scratch tiny pictures on to tablets of clay. The pictures stood for words. Over time, the letters we use today have grown from the early picture-writing.

△ The first writers were called scribes. They wrote standing up, or sitting on the floor.

## Alphabets and words

Only 26 different letters are used to make all the words in this book! These letters are called the alphabet. With this alphabet, we can write stories or poems, birthday cards or shopping lists. The same letters are used to make words in other languages, too.

▽ Some languages do not use the same alphabet. "Happy Birthday" in French is "Bon Anniversaire". But in Russian it is С днём рождения!

## A secret alphabet

Get together with your friends and make up an alphabet of your own. Decide on a new picture or symbol for each letter – perhaps you might draw an apple shape for the letter "a", and a banana shape for "b". Once you have made up a whole alphabet, you can write secret messages to each other!

S E C R E T

M E S S A G E

# The Earth

The Earth is a huge ball that spins round and round in space. Its surface is covered by water and land. If you could look down at the Earth from up in space, you would see lots of clouds swirling over its surface. Through the clouds you would see the blue colour of the oceans and seas. Nearly two-thirds of the Earth is covered with water. A layer of air, called the atmosphere, surrounds the Earth.

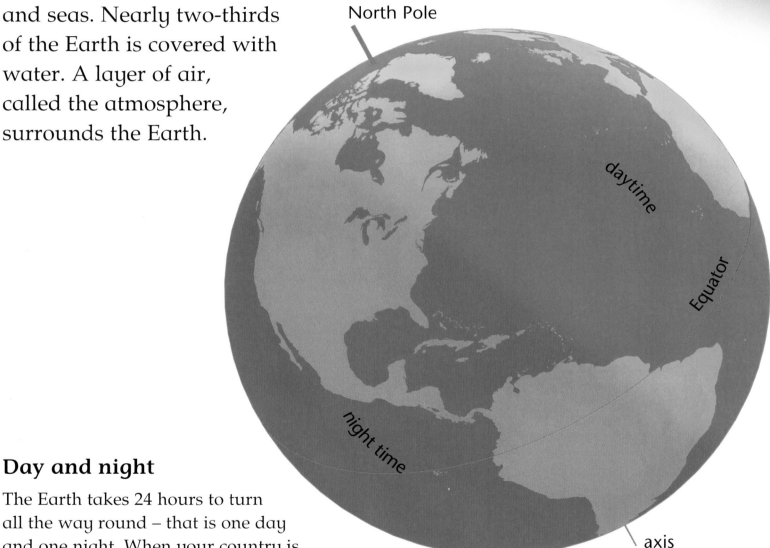

Sun's rays

North Pole

daytime

Equator

night time

axis

South Pole

△ The Earth always spins around an imaginary line through its middle that we call the Earth's axis. The axis runs through the North and South Poles. Right around the middle of the Earth on the outside is another imaginary line, called the Equator.

## Day and night

The Earth takes 24 hours to turn all the way round – that is one day and one night. When your country is facing the Sun, it is daytime for you. But as the Earth turns you away from the Sun, everything around you grows darker. During the darkness of the night, your country faces away from the Sun. When you wake up and everything is light again, this is a new day.

59

# Our world

From space, the Earth's surface looks smooth – but it isn't really. It has hills and valleys and mountains and gorges, even under the sea. This map is flat, but it shows the most important features on the Earth's surface.

▷ All the land in the world is divided up into seven big areas called "continents". They are Africa, Asia, Antarctica, Europe, North America, Oceania and South America. The continents are shown in different colours on the map.

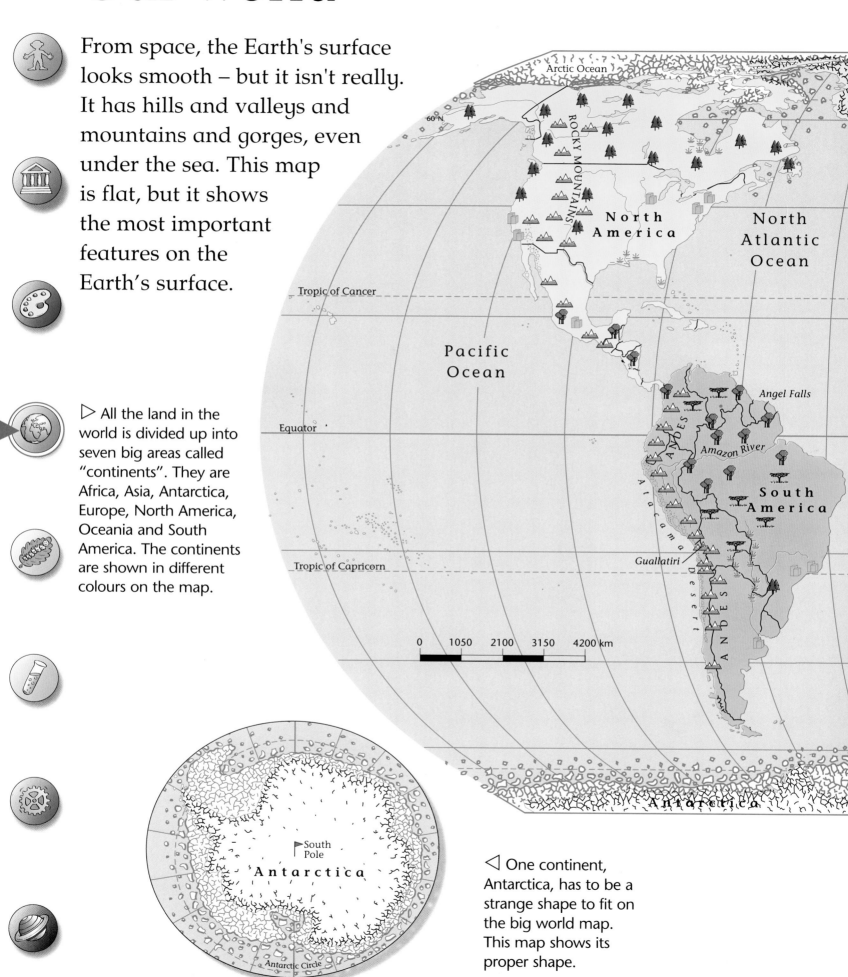

Arctic Ocean

60°N

ROCKY MOUNTAINS

North America

North Atlantic Ocean

Tropic of Cancer

Pacific Ocean

Equator

Angel Falls

ANDES

Amazon River

South America

Atacama Desert

Tropic of Capricorn

Guallatiri

ANDES

0   1050   2100   3150   4200 km

Antarctica

South Pole

Antarctica

Antarctic Circle

◁ One continent, Antarctica, has to be a strange shape to fit on the big world map. This map shows its proper shape.

Arctic Ocean

Arctic Circle

Europe

Asia

ALPS

CAUCASUS

Caspian Sea

Gobi Desert

Sahara Desert

River Nile

HIMALAYAS

Yangtze River

Tropic of Cancer

Mount Everest

Africa

Pacific Ocean

Indian Ocean

Equator

South Atlantic Ocean

Kalahari Desert

Great Victoria Desert

Tropic of Capricorn

Oceania

Southern Ocean

Antarctica

## Key

| | | | |
|---|---|---|---|
| desert | | high mountains | |
| marsh | | cold forest | |
| ice on land | | savannah | |
| ice on the sea | | hot forest | |
| country boundary | | very large cities | |

## Record breakers

Mount Everest is the highest mountain.
The Pacific is the biggest ocean.
The Nile is the longest river.
The Caspian Sea is the biggest lake.
Angel Falls is the highest waterfall.
Guallatiri is the highest volcano.
Greenland is the largest island.
The Sahara is the biggest desert.

# Sky above, Earth below

We live on the outside part of the Earth. Around and above us is the air we breathe. Beneath us is the Earth's crust, or outer layer. The crust is made of hard rocks, which have been wrinkled and bent to make mountains and valleys.

## Not so round

*The Earth is not really round. It is more like a slightly squashed ball. As the Earth spins, the middle part (around the Equator) bulges outwards. This makes the top and bottom parts (the poles) flatter.*

The crust is the Earth's outer layer. It is much thinner than the other layers.

Under the crust lies the mantle. The rocks in the mantle are red-hot, and some of them are so soft that they ooze about.

The rocks in the outer core are so hot that they have melted into a liquid.

The inner core lies at the centre of the Earth. The weight of all the rocks above the inner core squashes it into a solid ball.

## To the centre of the Earth

Can you dig right down to the centre of the Earth? If you tried, you would soon find it getting much too hot. As you go deeper, the rocks become hotter – and hotter! Scientists think that the very middle of the Earth is 60 times hotter than boiling water.

## A blanket of air

The Earth is wrapped up in an invisible layer of air called the atmosphere. Without this air, there would be no living things on Earth. The atmosphere acts like a blanket. It keeps us warm by trapping the heat of the Sun. And the air in the atmosphere contains important gases such as oxygen, which we breathe to keep us alive. The atmosphere also acts like sunglasses. It stops some of the Sun's harmful rays from reaching the ground.

satellite

△ We cannot explore deep inside the Earth, but we can travel up into the atmosphere, in balloons and aircraft.

The atmosphere has several different layers. Higher up, the air gets thinner and colder, and there is less oxygen to breathe. In the very highest layers there is hardly any air at all.

Space Shuttle

gas balloon

aeroplane

hot-air balloon

## Find out more about...

how people breathe on pages 14 to 15 (Lungs and breathing).

how water vapour changes into rain and snow on pages 68 to 69 (The weather).

# The moving Earth

Imagine what it would be like if the ground beneath your feet suddenly started to move! This is what happens during an earthquake. The top layer of the Earth bends and shakes. When a volcano erupts, it can be even more dramatic. Melted rock from under the surface bursts out through a crack in the Earth's crust in a red hot stream.

## Volcanoes

Deep under the Earth's surface are pockets of hot, melted rock. If there is a crack in the surface, this hot rock forces its way up and out of the crack. Tonnes of fiery, melted rock called "lava" blast out of the crack. As the lava flows away from the crack, it cools down and hardens into new rock. This new rock piles up around the crack to form a volcano.

▽ A cutaway picture of a volcano.

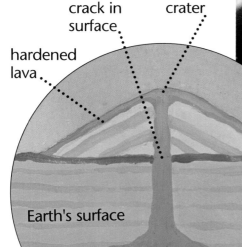

crack in surface

crater

hardened lava

Earth's surface

melted rock

▽ An erupting volcano is a terrifying sight. Lava bursts out from the top, and enormous clouds of ash and steam choke the air. Sometimes, a volcano can even explode and be completely blown apart.

## Earthquakes

When the Earth starts to shake violently, huge cracks open up in the Earth's surface. Buildings fall down and roads split apart. Bridges break in two and trees are ripped out of the ground. The land tilts and sends loose rock sliding downhill. Earthquakes under the sea can cause enormous waves that race to the shore and flood the land. These giant waves are called tsunamis.

### The biggest bang

*Over 100 years ago, in 1883, a volcanic island in Indonesia blew up. It was called Krakatau. The explosion of Krakatau made one of the loudest bangs ever. People heard it over 4800 kilometres away! A huge cloud of ash blotted out the sun for two whole days.*

△ A volcano may not erupt for many years, or it may stop erupting altogether. Thousands of years ago, this lake was part of a huge volcano. But the volcano stopped erupting, and now the crater where lava once poured out has filled with water.

# Shaping the landscape

We think of a mountain as something big and solid, and it always looks exactly the same. Yet a mountain is changing every day. Wind, cold and water are wearing it away, cutting and carving the rock into new shapes. All around us, the landscape is slowly changing. The land is always being worn away somewhere. At the same time, new land is being made somewhere else.

## Wearing away rocks

The weather can break down rocks in different ways. Water pours into cracks in the rock and freezes. The ice splits off small pieces of rock. Rivers cut away the land to make valleys and gorges. In hot dry places, the wind blows sand that scrapes away at rocks – just like sandpaper. And the sea's waves pull up pebbles and throw them at the cliffs, wearing away more rocks.

rain and ice wear away mountains

river carries away pieces of rock

cliffs are worn away by the sea

▷ This desert landscape in the USA is made up of soft rocks and hard rocks. Over millions of years, the soft rocks have been worn away more quickly than the hard rocks, leaving the hard rocks sticking up in strange shapes.

## Making new land

Although rocks are broken up, they do not vanish. Instead they are moved somewhere else. Rivers carry the rocks away, breaking them up into tiny pieces. The rivers flow into lakes and seas. Here, the rock pieces sink down to form a new layer of sand or mud. As time goes by, more and more layers build up on top of each other. This is how new land and rocks are formed.

new land forms in the river mouth

## Make a mountain

When two different pieces of the Earth's crust push into each other, their surfaces crumple and fold up. This is how mountains are made. You can see how this happens by using two big floppy books (try telephone directories). Put them on a table and push their open ends together. The pages will bend and fold. Some will be pushed downwards, and others upwards. It may look messy – but that is what mountains are!

### Find out more about . . .

rocks on pages 72 to 73 (Rocks, metals and minerals). ▶

# The weather

What's the weather like today? Is the sun shining, or is the sky full of clouds? Perhaps it is raining, or snowing. Weather can be so many different things – hot or cold, wet or dry, windy or still. And all this weather happens in the atmosphere, the layer of air around the Earth.

## Making rain

*If you fill the bath with hot water, clouds of steam (water vapour) rise up. When the steam touches something cold, like the window or the mirror, it cools down and turns back into a liquid. This is just what happens when water vapour rises up from the Earth.*

## The story of rain

Here is the story of how water from the sea becomes rain. The Sun warms up the water, which turns into a gas called water vapour. Wind carries the vapour up into the sky. Here the air is cooler, and the vapour turns into tiny water droplets. These join together to make a cloud. Over high ground, the air gets cooler still. Soon, the droplets grow so heavy that they fall to the ground as rain.

water vapour makes clouds in cooler air

WIND

water vapour rises

sea water

## Snow

At the very top of a cloud, the air may be very cold. Here, the water vapour freezes into crystals of ice. These delicate crystals stick together to form flakes of snow. When the snowflakes are heavy enough, they fall towards the ground.

## Thunder and lightning

After very hot weather we may have a thunderstorm. Tall black clouds appear in the sky. They contain a powerful charge of electricity. When the clouds move close together, or near the ground, giant sparks of electricity fly between them. These are flashes of lightning. Thunder is the noise made by the hot air expanding around the sparks.

droplets get heavier

RAIN

rainwater runs back to the sea in rivers and streams

## Why does wind blow?

The layer of air presses down on the Earth. When the Sun shines, it warms up the Earth. The Earth, in turn, warms the air above it. Warm air does not press down so hard. It starts to rise, and cooler air rushes in to take its place underneath. This is what causes wind.

▽ Wind can blow at many different speeds. Here are some ways of describing them, starting with a calm (no wind at all).

calm

light breeze

strong breeze

gale

hurricane

69

# Climates and seasons

Is it usually cold where you live? Or is it hot and sunny? Some places have a lot of warm sun and not much rain. Some have a lot of sunshine and rain. Other places are cold all year round. Each part of the world has its own special mixture of weather during the year. This mixture is called the climate of that region.

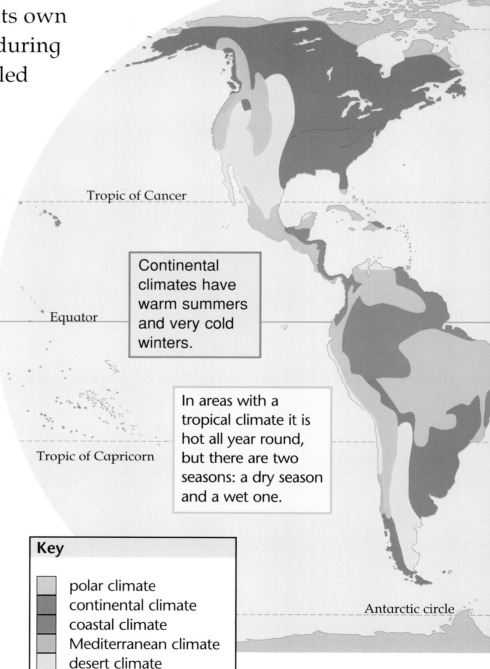

▷ This forest in northern America has a coastal climate – warm summers, mild winters and rain all year. In autumn, the leaves change colour and fall from the trees.

## The seasons

In most places the weather changes throughout the year. We call these changes the seasons. In some parts of the world, there are only one or two seasons. But in other places there are four seasons – spring, summer, autumn and winter.

Tropic of Cancer

Equator

Continental climates have warm summers and very cold winters.

In areas with a tropical climate it is hot all year round, but there are two seasons: a dry season and a wet one.

Tropic of Capricorn

Antarctic circle

△ Hardly any rain falls on this African desert, and few plants grow. Desert climates are always very dry.

**Key**

- polar climate
- continental climate
- coastal climate
- Mediterranean climate
- desert climate
- tropical climate
- equatorial climate

- high mountains

▷ The Mediterranean area is hot and dry in the summer. Winters are rainy, but it is still warm.

▽ In the Asian rainforest, heavy rain and heat make the plants grow very quickly. Climates on the Equator have only one season – hot and wet.

Arctic circle

Equator

Equator

Antarctic circle

△ In Antarctica, it is cold all year round. The snow and ice never melt. The North and South Poles have two seasons: a long, cold winter and a short summer.

## ! Sizzling icebergs

Antarctica, at the South Pole, is the coldest place on Earth today. But it once had a very hot climate. Millions of years ago, Antarctica was actually on the Equator!

# Rocks, metals and minerals

Rocks are all around you! Look for them on paths and roads, on the beach, in fields and streams, and in walls and houses. There are many different kinds of rock. They can be hard or crumbly, rough or smooth, shiny or dull. Rocks are a mixture of metals and other solid materials called minerals. Many of these metals and minerals are very useful to us.

## Changing rocks

Rocks are millions of years old. Yet they are changing all the time, as the surface of the Earth changes. As some rocks are worn away by the weather, other new rocks are being made. These changes take millions of years.

△ Some rocks start as a red-hot liquid, deep inside the Earth. The liquid bursts out onto the surface through a volcano. When it cools, the liquid hardens to form rock.

△ Other rocks are formed from mud, sand or tiny pieces of broken shells. These settle in layers at the bottom of rivers, lakes or seas. As the layers slowly get thicker, the sand or mud gets squashed into rock.

△ Rocks can also be changed without being broken up first. If rocks become very hot or are squeezed and heated at the same time, they may change into a different kind of rock. These kind of changes often happen when mountains are being formed.

## Rocks in your home

An amazing number of things in your home came originally from rocks. Metals are made from special types of rock called "ore". Your bike is probably made of steel, which comes from iron ore. All your cups, bowls and plates, and the wash basin in your bathroom, are made of ceramics. Ceramics come from clay, which is another kind of rock.

glass-making sand

limestone

△ Glass is made from special sand and a type of rock called limestone.

iron ore

## Animal and plant fuel

The oil and petrol that we use in our cars are made from animals! Oil is formed from the squashed bodies of animals and plants buried millions of years ago. The oil soaks into the rocks around it, like water into a sponge.

## Buried treasure

Some metals and minerals are easy to find in the ground. Others are much harder. Gold and silver are rare metals. Diamonds and rubies are rare minerals. They are called precious metals and stones, and are very valuable.

△ This beautiful sword has precious metals and jewels (precious stones) in the handle.

### Find out more about...

mountain-building on pages 66 to 67 (Shaping the landscape).

animals that lived millions of years ago on pages 80 to 81 (Prehistoric life).

how we use oil on pages 116 to 117 (Everything needs energy).

# Earth in danger

The Earth is under attack – not from space aliens, but from people like us! Many of the things we do are damaging the world. People are cutting down too many trees, burning too much fuel and spreading too many dangerous chemicals.

These activities are harming the Earth's animals and plants. They also harm the air we breathe and the water we drink.

heat from the Sun

escaping heat

layer of dirty air

trapped heat

harmful gases

## Warming up

The air around the Earth is getting dirtier. This is because we are burning too much fuel. We fill the air with harmful gases and dirt, which makes a change in the air. The layer of dirty air around the Earth begins to trap more of the Sun's heat than before, and the Earth becomes a warmer place.

*Find out more about...*

disappearing animals on page 94 (Animals in danger).

## Acid rain

Cars, lorries and factory chimneys give out gases that are full of harmful chemicals. These gases rise into the air. Here they mix with rain droplets, and turn them into acid rain. When this acid rain falls to the ground, it harms plants, especially trees. It also damages buildings.

▷ This pine tree has lost all its needles because of acid rain.

# Animals and Plants

People are not the only living things on the Earth. We share it with many millions of other animals and plants. They live in every part of the world, from the bottom of the deepest ocean to the top of the highest mountain. Some plants and animals are huge. Others are so tiny that you need a microscope to see them.

The lives of animals and plants join together in a complicated way that we call "the balance of nature". A snail eats a leaf. A bird eats the snail. A fox eats the bird. Each one depends on the other for food.

# How plants grow

Wherever you live, you will find plants. Some are grown specially by farmers to give us food, timber and other useful materials. But most plants are wild. There are thousands of different kinds of wild plants, growing in many different places: hot, dry deserts, damp forests, under ice and snow – even in cities!

## Parts of a plant

Plants that produce flowers are called "flowering plants". Each part of the plant has an important job to do. The roots take up water, and hold the plant firmly in the ground. The stem supports the leaves, flowers and fruit. The leaves make the plant's food, and the flowers make fruits and seeds. One day, the seeds will start to grow into new plants.

▷ Plants can make their own food. All they need is air, water and sunlight. They use sunlight to turn water and a gas called carbon dioxide from the air into a sugary food called sap. This happens inside the leaves. The sap travels through the plant's stems, from the leaves to wherever the plant needs food.

flower

fruit

seed

sunlight

water

carbon dioxide

stem

leaf

sap

root

## Flowers and seeds

The reason plants have flowers is to help pass tiny grains called pollen from one plant to another. The plants need this pollen to make seeds. In some flowers, the pollen is blown from place to place by the wind. Other flowers get insects to carry their pollen for them. With the help of the pollen, the flower can make seeds.

◁ The sweet smell and bright colour of many flowers attract insects. The insects come to collect delicious nectar from inside the flower. As the insect drinks the nectar, tiny grains of pollen stick to its body. When the insect visits another flower, it leaves some pollen behind.

## All kinds of plants

Not all plants have flowers. Plants come in all shapes and sizes, from tiny mosses to huge trees. Here are some of the many other kinds of plant.

◁ Trees like this monkey-puzzle tree have a tall, straight trunk and thin leaves like needles. They make their seeds inside woody cones.

▽ A moss is a very simple kind of plant. It has no flowers. It makes tiny, dust-like spores instead of seeds.

▷ A mushroom is a kind of fungus. It never has flowers. It gets its food from dead plant material in the soil.

## Grow plants from seeds

*It is easy to grow your own plants. All you need is a saucer, some kitchen paper towels and a packet of seeds (mustard and cress seeds are the easiest). Soak the paper towels in water and put them on the saucer. Then sprinkle the seeds on top, and put the saucer on a sunny window-sill. Make sure the towels stay damp. Your seeds will soon start to sprout.*

## Find out more about...

plants that we eat on pages 40 to 41 (What we eat).

77

# Animal families

**Mammals** are the only animals with fur or hair on their bodies. All mammals drink milk from their mothers when they are young. Bats, whales and monkeys are mammals – and so are you!

**Birds** are the only animals with feathers. They are born from eggs with hard shells. Birds have strong wings in the same place that you have arms. Not all birds can fly. Ostriches can only walk or run, while penguins use their wings for swimming.

Most **reptiles** live on dry land. Their skin is covered with tough, dry scales. We say that reptiles are "cold-blooded" because the temperature of their body depends on their surroundings. Lizards, snakes, crocodiles and turtles are all reptiles.

**Amphibians** are born in the water, but when they are grown up they can live on land. Like reptiles, they are cold-blooded animals. Frogs, toads and newts are all amphibians.

**Fish** live in water. Their bodies are covered in scales, and they have fins to help them swim. Fish can breathe underwater. They have special parts called gills which take oxygen from the water.

Animals come in lots of shapes and sizes. Some are furry and some are scaly. Some have hard shells and some have feathers. Some animals are enormous, like the blue whale, and some are tiny, like the flea. Scientists think that altogether, there are more than 10 million different kinds, or species, of animal!

## Animal groups

Scientists have made it easier for us to tell one animal from another. They have arranged animals that are similar to each other into groups, in the same way that books about the same subject are put together on a library shelf. Above are some of the main animal groups.

## Worms and more worms

There are more roundworms than any other kind of animal. These tiny worms live in the sea and on land. Scientists believe that there are at least 40,000,000,000,000,000,000,000,000 of them!

## Can you find these creatures?

| | |
|---|---|
| butterfly | ostrich |
| catfish | rat |
| crab | shark |
| crocodile | snail |
| elephant | snake |
| frog | spider |
| millipede | surgeon fish (a kind |
| newt | of flatfish) |
| octopus | swallow |

## Arthropods

do not have bones inside them. Instead, they have a hard skin or shell that covers the outside of their body. Arthropods have at least three pairs of legs. Insects are the most common arthropods, and there are 8 million different kinds of insect!

## Molluscs have

a soft body, with a hard shell around it. Some, like the clam, have two shells. Molluscs have no legs, but many have a kind of "foot" to help them move about. An octopus is a mollusc with its shell inside its body.

## Find out more about...

the bones inside us on pages 12 to 13 (Bones and muscles).

how we breathe on pages 14 to 15 (Lungs and breathing).

# Prehistoric life

Long ago, there were no people on the Earth. There were no animals at all. Very slowly, over millions of years, the first living things developed. They were made of just one tiny cell. These living things gradually changed and grew bigger. They became plants and animals, and lived in the sea. Some animals grew legs and began to live on land. Many different kinds of animals developed. Soon they filled every part of the Earth.

## The beginning of life

Among the first creatures were simple water plants called algae. Later plants began to grow on land. Giant ferns and horsetails covered much of the world. The first animals were tiny sea creatures, with tails for swimming. Then animals became bigger, and grew bony skeletons. The first land animals were amphibians, which were followed by reptiles (including dinosaurs). Mammals and birds were the last kinds of animals to appear.

3000

single-cell animals

2000

algae

1000

jellyfish

trilobites

giant ferns

first fish with jaws

500

first amphibians

first reptiles

400

first dinosaurs

flying insects

300

first mammals

200

first birds

first apes

first humans

100

present day

80

# Age of the dinosaurs

Dinosaurs were the most successful kind of early animal. The word dinosaur means "terrible lizard". Some dinosaurs were enormous. *Brachiosaurus* was as big as five elephants! Some, such as *Tyrannosaurus rex*, were very fierce. Other dinosaurs were only the size of a cat or dog. The age of the dinosaurs lasted for a long time, but the last ones died out millions of years ago.

▷ How do we know what dinosaurs looked like? After all, they died long before the first people lived on Earth. But the dinosaurs did not completely disappear. The skeletons of some of them turned into rock. These rocky remains are called "fossils".

▷ The pterosaur had wings to help it fly or glide.

▽ The stegosaur had bony plates along its back.

▽ The apatosaur was a giant dinosaur with a long neck and a small head. It ate plants.

▽ The plesiosaur lived in the sea and ate fish.

◁ The tyrannosaur had huge sharp teeth. It hunted other animals and ate them.

## ! Dinosaurs are alive!

*Dinosaurs may be dead, but some closely related animals are still alive. Crocodiles, lizards and snakes are all part of the dinosaur family. And birds may really be flying dinosaurs!*

▷ *Deinonychus* was a frightening hunter. Its name means "terrible claw".

# Wildlife in a town

A town or city does not seem to be a good place for watching wildlife. Towns are mostly made of stone or brick or concrete. They are full of lorries and buses and crowds of people. Yet many plants and animals are able to live here. If you look carefully, you will be surprised at how much wildlife you can see!

## Birds' nests

Birds do not always live in trees and hedges. House-martins make their mud nests under the edge of a roof, while coal tits like nesting boxes. Can you spot these nests?

squirrel

robin

wren

chaffinch

tit

sparrow

blackbird

◁ Many foxes live in wild corners of towns and cities. They come into the town centre at night. Finding food in dustbins or on rubbish tips is much easier for the fox than hunting small animals and birds.

82

## Animals in your home

A surprising number of animals live in your home without you knowing it! Most are too tiny for you to see, but you may find some if you look carefully. Mice, cockroaches and flies like houses because they are warm and it is easy to find food. Spiders spin webs in dark corners, while beetle grubs bore holes in wood.

△ Wood-boring beetle grubs like this one live in wood for two years or more before they become adults.

## Insect hunt

*Here is a good way to watch animals in the garden. Find a stone and turn it over. What creatures can you see? How many legs have they got? What are they doing? Remember to put the stone back afterwards.*

dragonfly

poppy

buddleia

rosebay willowherb

▷ City gardens and parks are full of beautiful plants. Plants grow in all sorts of other places too. Waste ground or railway embankments are ideal places for wild plants such as rosebay willowherb. People grow buddleia bushes in their gardens, but they also spring up in cracks in pavements and walls, and sometimes even on roofs.

# Wildlife in a meadow

When you lie down in a grass meadow, you are in the middle of a miniature world. It looks like a jungle, with a tangle of grass stems, leaves and roots. All around you insects are busy searching for food. Crickets munch on young grass. Tiger beetles hunt for ants. Up above, bumble bees collect sugary nectar from the flowers. Field mice, rabbits and birds are here too – they seem like giants!

## An ants' nest

A huge number of ants live inside an ants' nest. But it is started by just one ant – the queen. The queen ant lays her eggs under the ground. They hatch and become ant grubs, which grow into worker ants. The workers build the nest and gather food, while the queen goes on and on laying eggs. In the end, the nest may contain over 100,000 ants!

1 queen ant
2 worker ants
3 eggs
4 grubs
5 food

## Fast food

Rabbits love to nibble grass and other green plants. But grass is tough food. It takes a long time to break down, or digest. So the rabbit eats it twice! First, the chewed grass passes out of the rabbit's body as little pellets. Then the rabbit eats the pellets. This way, it gets twice as much goodness from the grass.

## Danger above

High above the meadow flies the kestrel. This bird is a meat-eater. It hunts for small animals such as voles or mice. The kestrel can hover in the air and stay in one place, even in a strong wind. When it spots a mouse, it swoops down very quickly and grabs the animal with its strong feet.

## Moles

The mole digs long tunnels under the ground. It pushes the earth up to the surface, making mounds that we call molehills. These tunnels are not just a home for the mole - they are traps, too. Earthworms fall down into them and provide an easy meal. Sometimes there are so many worms that the mole stores them for later.

## Frantic Fliers

Some insects have to work very hard to fly. A butterfly beats its wings about 10 times each second. The tiny midge beats its wings 1,000 times a second!

# Wildlife on the grasslands

The grassland, or savannah, of East Africa looks bare and dry, but it is full of food. Plant-eating animals like giraffes and elephants chew the leaves or twigs of trees. Herds of zebra and gazelle feed on the grass. But there are also meat-eaters here. Lions and cheetahs hunt the zebras and gazelles. Any meat they leave is quickly finished up by jackals and vultures.

△ Giraffes are the tallest animals in the world. They use their long necks to feed from the highest branches of trees, where other animals cannot reach.

wildebeeste

locust

secretary bird

## Grass: the wonder plant

Savannah grass sometimes grows as tall as 3 metres. It provides food for many animals, big and small. Zebras eat the top part of the grass. Wildebeeste eat the leafy centre. Gazelles eat the short, young shoots. Birds eat the grass seeds. Beetles munch the dead leaves.

oxpecker

gazelle

lion

zebra

△ Big brown mounds stick up out of the flat land. They are twice as tall as a person! Yet these mounds are built by millions of tiny termites, as a city to live in. The mounds are so strong that few animals can damage them.

△ Would you like an oxpecker on your back? Its sharp claws would dig into you as you walked along. But zebras do not mind giving this bird a lift. This is because the oxpeckers eat up the tiny, itchy insects called ticks which burrow under the zebras' skins.

## Speedy cheetahs

*The cheetah is the fastest of all land animals. With its long legs and slim body, it is built for speed. It can run at more than 80 kilometres an hour, for short bursts. At that speed, it can easily catch a gazelle or an antelope.*

# Wildlife in a woodland

This forest is in northern USA. Most of the trees here have broad, flat leaves, so they are called broadleaf trees! They are home for many different birds and insects. Larger animals shelter or hide in the shade beneath the trees. In summer, the millions of leaves block out most of the sunlight. But in autumn the leaves fall, and the forest becomes more light and open.

▷ A broadleaf tree makes a perfect snack bar for many kinds of bird. Warblers and blue jays hunt for insects and caterpillars. The sapsucker drills holes in the tree with its beak, then drinks the juicy sap. The acorn woodpecker drills holes, too. It uses them to store acorns and berries for the winter.

woodpecker

sapsucker

## Falling leaves

In autumn the weather gets colder. The leaves of the broadleaf trees change colour. and fall to the ground. Next spring, the trees will grow new leaves. Meanwhile, the piles of fallen leaves start to rot away. Millions of tiny worms and beetles live here. They chew up the leaves and help to mix them with the soil.

raccoon

earwig

earthworm

millipede

ground beetle

blue jay

opossum

warbler

white-tailed deer

skunk

▽ Black bears spend most of winter fast asleep. They curl up in a snug cave or hidden hollow. While they sleep, their bodies use less energy. This helps them to live through the cold months, when there is little food.

## A butterfly grows up

A butterfly starts life as an egg. After a few days, the egg hatches. A tiny caterpillar crawls out. The caterpillar feeds on leaves. It grows bigger and bigger. When it is big enough, the caterpillar grows a brown shell, called a pupa. Inside the pupa, the caterpillar changes. At last, the pupa splits open and out comes a butterfly!

purple hairsteak butterfly

eggs

caterpillar

pupa

**!**

## Stinky skunk

*The skunk is one of the smelliest animals in the world. If it is attacked, it turns round and squirts a horrible, stinky liquid from near its bottom!*

harpy eagle

# Wildlife in the rainforest

Imagine you are standing in the middle of a rainforest in South America. All around you, huge trees tower up towards the sky. At the very top, the trees end in a mass of leaves. Beneath the leaves it is dark and very hot. It rains here almost every day, so the air is damp. Because the rainforest is hot and wet, it is an ideal place for plants. Huge numbers of vines, ferns and flowers cover the trees. Insects, birds and climbing animals live up among the leaves.

In fact, rainforests are home to more plants and animals than any other place in the world.

## Life on high

You will not see many animals on the ground. Most of them live high up in the tree tops. This is called the canopy. Up here, there is plenty of food. The rainforest is always warm, so the trees grow new leaves, fruits and seeds throughout the year.

▽ The arrow-poison frog grows up in a pond up a tree! The mother frog carries her tadpoles on her back through the leaves until she sees a plant called a bromeliad. Its cup-shaped leaves catch rainwater. The frog puts her tadpoles into the water, where they can grow up in their own private pool.

▽ The spider monkey swings through the branches. It uses its tail as well as its arms and legs.

▽ The macaw cracks nuts with its tough bill.

▽ The sloth hangs upside down from a branch, and moves very slowly.

▽ The tiny hummingbird sips nectar from flowers through its long bill.

## A cat that can fish!

The jaguar loves to eat fish. It catches them just like a fisherman. The jaguar puts the tip of its tail in the water. Fish swim up to look at the twitching tail – and in a flash the jaguar turns and grabs them!

▽ Some rainforest animals are very hard to spot, because their shape and colour make them look like something else. Leaf insects are green, and their bodies look just like leaves. This helps them to hide from their enemies.

## Tree supports

Some rainforest trees are as tall as an apartment block. But their roots do not go down very deep, and so do not support the tree well. If the top of a tree is very heavy, it may fall over in a storm. Some kinds of tree have roots called buttresses. These stick out from the trunk and prop it up.

potto

buttress roots

# Wildlife in the desert

The Sahara in Africa is the biggest desert in the world. It is as big as the USA! Most of the Sahara is bare and dry, with scattered rocks, gravel or plain sand. It hardly ever rains. During the day it is very hot, but at night it quickly cools down. Animals and plants have to live with little water, and they must survive the fierce heat of the sun.

## Keeping cool

Very few animals move about during the day. The heat of the sun would dry out their bodies. Mammals, such as the fennec fox and the gerbil, hide under rocks and in burrows. In these shady places it is much cooler. As soon as the sun goes down, the animals come out to hunt for food.

▽ The fennec fox uses its huge ears to keep cool. The thin ear flaps contain many tiny blood vessels close to the surface. As blood moves through these vessels, the fox loses its warmth to the outside air.

sand grouse

# Animals and Plants

▷ The sand grouse has to fly a long way to find water. But its young cannot fly. How do they get a drink? The adult sand grouse has spongy feathers on its front. It soaks these feathers in water, then flies home. The young suck the water from the feathers.

cactus

▷ Sand is hard to walk on, and during the day it becomes scorching hot. But desert creatures still find ways to move about. The sidewinder snake moves along sideways. Only a small part of its body touches the sand at a time. The skink swims through the sand by wriggling its body.

sidewinder

esparto grass

△ Plants need water to live and grow. But in the desert there is hardly any moisture. So desert plants have special ways of keeping water. Some store it in their stems or roots. The leaves of esparto grass curl up so that they are shaded from the sun.

skink

## ❗ What a thirst!

*The camel can walk for several days in the desert without drinking at all. But at the end of that time, it will drink as much as 180 litres of water – that is the same as 540 cans of drink!*

# Wildlife in Arctic lands

Winter is very long in the Arctic lands called tundra. For nine months the ground is frozen, and covered in ice and snow. During most of that time, there is no sun at all. But in March the sun appears at last and the short summer begins. The heat melts the surface of the frozen ground, forming pools and bogs. Over the next few weeks, plants flower, insects lay eggs and animals hurry to mate and find food. Soon winter will be here again.

Arctic tern

caribou

Arctic fox

## Summer visitors

Many animals come to the tundra just for the summer, when there is plenty of food. Caribou arrive in huge herds to feed on leaves and tiny plants called lichens. Birds come to eat the mosquitoes and other insects which hatch in the boggy pools. But the Arctic tern travels furthest of all. It rears its young near the North Pole, then flies right across the world to Antarctica for the southern summer.

△ The Arctic willow is one of the few trees on the tundra. It does not grow upwards, but sideways. This keeps it close to the ground, sheltered from the icy winds.

◁ In winter, the Arctic fox grows a special new coat. It is thick, to keep out the cold, and white, so that the fox is difficult to see against the snow. In summer, its coat turns brown again. Other animals, such as the Arctic hare and the ptarmigan, also have white winter coats.

◁ Musk oxen can move quickly, but they do not run away from packs of hunting wolves. Instead, the oxen stand in a circle with their long curved horns facing outwards. Their young shelter in the centre of the circle, safe from the wolves.

▽ Lemmings spend the harsh winters safe in burrows under the snow. Here, they look for leaves, roots and stems to eat. In summer, when the snow melts, they dig burrows in the hard ground. But outside their burrows, they must beware of snowy owls and other fierce hunters.

# Wildlife in the ocean

The waters of the South Pacific are warm and full of light. Many wonderful creatures live here – coloured fishes, sea urchins, giant squid, sea slugs and sharks. But the most wonderful of all are the corals. Corals are tiny animals, which build themselves houses of limestone. Over many years, their stone houses have built up into huge coral reefs.

▽ The squid looks clumsy, but can move very fast – it is jet-propelled! It fills itself up with water, then squirts the water out through a tube. This water "jet" sends the squid shooting along.

great white shark

jacks

squid

elkhorn coral

green turtle

sea fan

sea cucumber

stonefish

stagshorn coral

## Food for giants

The sea is full of tiny plants and animals – so tiny that you can hardly see them without a microscope. This mixture of creatures is called plankton. Plankton is a vital source of food for many other animals, from shrimps to jellyfish. The biggest eaters of plankton are whales. The blue whale is the largest animal in the world, but it lives on tiny plankton.

box jellyfish

spectacled porpoise

## Coral giant

The biggest coral reef of all is the Great Barrier Reef, east of Australia. There is enough stone in the coral here to build one of the great Egyptian pyramids – 8 million times over!

hammerhead shark

◁ What is a shark? You may think it is a big fierce fish with sharp teeth, like the great white shark. But sharks come in all shapes and sizes. Some, like the hammerhead, look very odd. Others do not look like sharks at all! The wobbegong is flat, and lies on the seabed waiting for food.

wobbegong

fusilier fish

brain coral

▷ The sea anemone has special stinging tentacles. It uses these to catch small fish. But the clown fish does not get stung or eaten. It lives among the anemone's tentacles, safe from other enemies. The anenome benefits too – it eats food scraps left over from the clown fish's meals.

anemone

clown fish

sea slug

# Animals in danger

Have you ever seen a dodo? Or a quagga? It is not likely because these animals are extinct. This means that every one of them has died – there are none left in the world. Thousands of different animal and plant species have become extinct. Many disappeared quite naturally long ago. Others are in danger today, because people hunt them, or because we are changing the places where these animals and plants live.

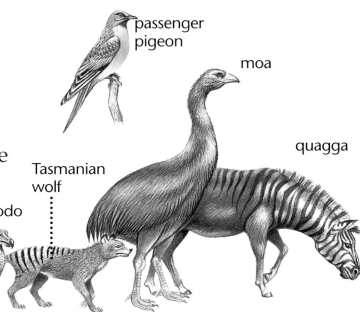

passenger pigeon

moa

quagga

Tasmanian wolf

dodo

△ All of these animals have died out – mainly because of what people have done. Hunters have killed some of them. Farmers, loggers and builders have taken away the homes and food supplies of others.

▽ These are just a few of the many animals that are in danger of extinction today.

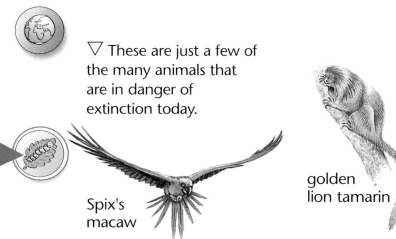

golden lion tamarin

Spix's macaw

## What you can do

In some places, things are slowly changing for the better. Many animals are now protected, and there are special reserves where they can live safely. You can help to look after wildlife, too. In your local area there are probably groups that help to save endangered species. You could join one of these groups, or get in touch with the World Wide Fund For Nature, which helps wildlife all over the world. Its address is Panda House, Weyside Park, Godalming, Surrey, GU7 1XR.

mountain gorilla

giant panda

tiger

blue whale

*Find out more about . . .*

damage to our Earth on page 74 (Earth in danger).

# Science

Science helps us to understand how the world is made, and how it works. All through history, scientists have tried to find the answers to many questions. What are things made of? What happens when something becomes hot or cold? How do light and sound travel? Where does energy come from? Scientists have found lots of answers, but there are still plenty of questions left.

# What is everything made of?

Everything in the world is made of something. This "something" is called matter. You are made of matter – and so is everything else, from mountains to ice creams. Even the air you breathe is made of matter. All this matter comes in one of three states – as a solid, as a liquid or as a gas.

## The three states

The waterfall, the rocks and the wind moving the clouds in this picture are all very different kinds of matter. The rock is hard, and has a fixed shape. We call it a solid. The waterfall is made of water, and has no fixed shape. It is a liquid. The wind is made of air, which is a gas. A gas will fill any space it is put into.

## Changing states

*Matter does not always stay the same. It can change from one state to another. A solid can become a liquid, and a liquid can become a gas. It is easy to see these changes with water.*

*Ice is solid water. If you heat a piece of ice, it melts and turns into a liquid.*

heat

ice cube (solid)

water (liquid)

*If you heat the water more, it boils and turns into steam. The steam is a gas.*

steam (gas)

100

# Changing shapes

We can make many useful objects by heating materials to melt them, then changing their shape before they cool down again. Metals such as iron or gold are solid, but when they are heated a lot they melt and become liquids. This hot liquid is poured into shaped moulds. When it cools down, it becomes a solid in the shape of the mould.

## Frying tonight

*Heating a liquid can turn it into a solid! The next time you have fried eggs, watch them being cooked. The egg is runny when it goes into the pan, but as it gets hot, it turns solid. This is a different sort of change from when something melts, because the egg stays solid when it cools down.*

◁ These workers are pouring very hot metal into moulds. Their silver suits and special visors (masks) help to protect them from the heat.

## Find out more about...

water and the weather on pages 68 and 69 (The weather).

making new materials on pages 116 and 117 (Making materials).

# Building blocks

We know that everything is made of matter. But what is matter made of? Imagine that you could chop an iron bar into little pieces. Then imagine chopping one of those pieces into even tinier bits. If you kept cutting the smaller and smaller pieces, eventually you would have the tiniest bits of all. These are called atoms. All matter is made from atoms.

◁ This part of the salt grain has been magnified even further, to show the atoms. There are two sorts in salt – sodium and chlorine.

## Millions of atoms

A pile of salt contains millions of tiny grains of salt. It is easy to see one salt grain, but just one of these grains contains millions of atoms. The atoms are so tiny that you cannot see them.

△ The oblong shapes in this photograph are grains of salt. The photo has been made many times bigger to help you see the grains more clearly. Even so, the salt atoms are too small to see.

▽ Each of these building blocks has the name of an element on it.

## What are elements?

Atoms are not all the same. There are about 100 different kinds. A piece of matter which is made from just one kind of atom is called an element. So there are about 100 different elements.

Elements are the "building blocks" for all other kinds of matter. They can be put together in different ways to make millions of kinds of matter.

102

## How we use matter

Matter comes in many different forms. It can be hard or soft, heavy or light. You can see through some kinds of matter (like air), but not through others (like coal). A bicycle contains lots of different kinds of matter. Each one has a special use for the rider.

this plastic is tough and light

this plastic is flexible and waterproof

cotton is soft but keeps in the warmth

glass is clear

metal is strong

rubber is soft and bendy

! **Amazing atoms**

*More than a million atoms would fit on to the thickness of one human hair!*

### The hardest

Diamonds are the hardest material in the world. Scientists are trying to make a new kind of glass with a diamond coating. This glass will be so hard that you could never scratch it.

△ These diamonds are on a piece of kimberlite, which is the rock that diamonds are found in.

*Find out more about...*

how we make materials on pages 116 to 117 (Making materials).

# Everything needs energy

You need energy to keep you going. Without it, your body cannot walk, run, breathe or even think! You get your energy from food. Other things need energy to keep going, too. Animals get energy from food, like us. Plants get their energy from the Sun. A car gets energy from petrol. A television gets energy from electricity. A sailing ship gets energy from the wind.

## Making things happen

There are many different sources of energy, even around your home. You cannot always see where the energy is coming from. Anything that moves or changes is using energy from somewhere.

sunlight helps the plants to grow.

petrol makes the car work

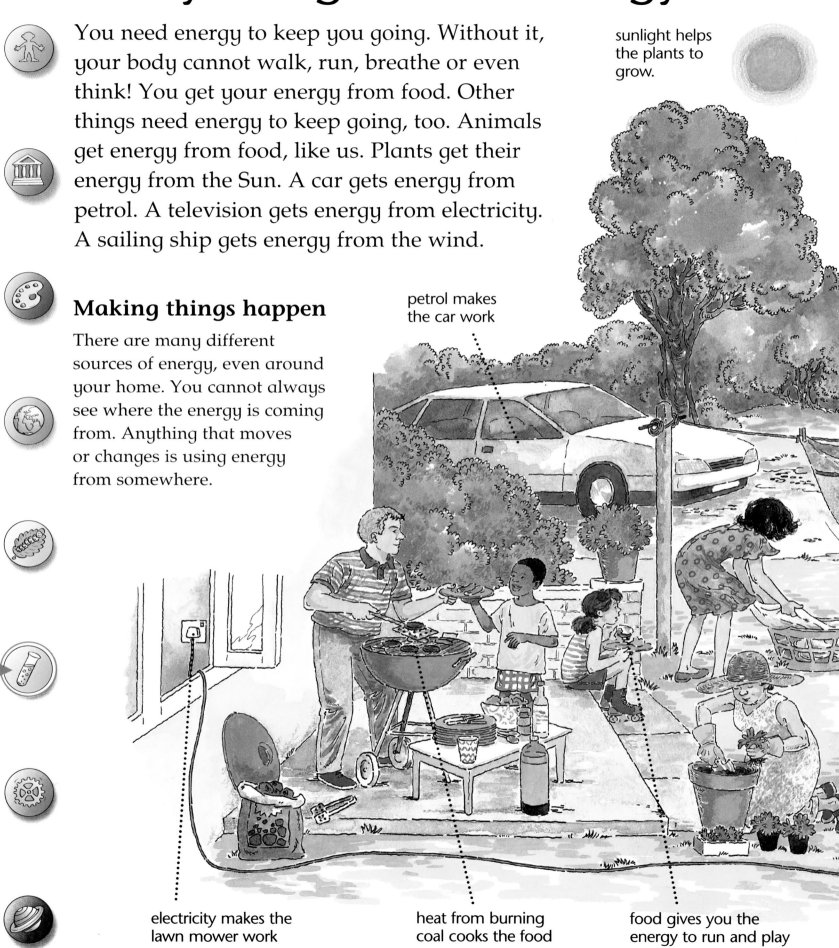

electricity makes the lawn mower work

heat from burning coal cooks the food

food gives you the energy to run and play

## Storing energy

Energy from the Sun can be stored away and used later. One of these stored sources of energy is oil. It is made from tiny plants and animals that were squashed together over millions of years. Petrol and other fuels come from oil. So cars, lorries, aircraft and ships all use energy from very old animals and plants!

wind keeps the kite in the air and dries the wet clothes

**!**

## Pedal power

The energy from one litre of petrol will drive a car about 16 kilometres. If you use the same amount of energy on a bicycle, you could cycle over 500 kilometres!

## The energy factory

Where does energy come from? Most of it starts in one place – the Sun. Heat and light from the Sun travel through space to the Earth. Grass and other plants use the Sun's energy to grow. Then cows and other animals eat the grass. Cows turn some of the energy from the grass into milk. If you drink the milk, the energy passes into your body.

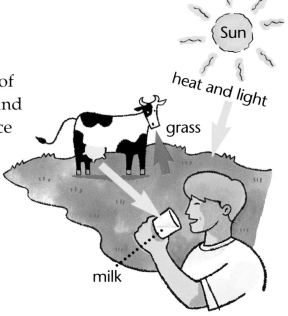

Sun

heat and light

grass

milk

## Find out more about . . .

energy from electricity on pages 112 to 113 (Electricity).

# Pushing and pulling

All around you, things are being pushed or pulled. When you kick a ball, you are pushing it. When a crane lifts a heavy load, it pulls it into the air. Pushes and pulls are forces. Forces can make objects speed up, slow down or change the direction they move in.

## Body force

You can use the muscles in your body to produce a force. When you pick up a spoon, the muscles in your arm pull on the bones to make the arm bend. Weightlifters have very strong muscles. They can pick up much heavier things than spoons!

▽ As the weightlifter begins to lift, he pulls on the bar to get it off the floor.

▷ Once he has got the weights to his chest, the weightlifter gives a huge push to lift the bar above his head.

**!** *Big lift*
*Andrey Chermenkin of Russia lifted a world record 260 kilograms in a weightlifting contest in 1996. This is like lifting almost four full-grown men above your head at the same time!*

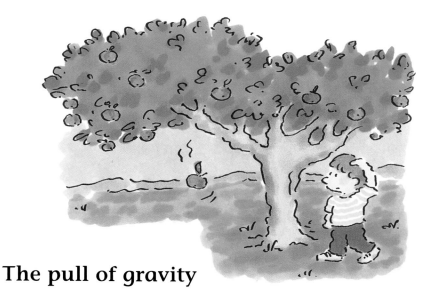

## The pull of gravity

If you drop a stone, it falls to the ground. A special force is pulling the stone downwards, towards the centre of the Earth. We call this force gravity. Everything on Earth is pulled down by gravity. Even when you stand still, the gravity of the Earth is pulling you downwards. Without it you would float in the air!

## The force of friction

If you sit down on a grassy slope, you won't slide down it. This is because a force called friction stops you. The surface of your clothes and the grass are both rough. They catch on each other, and stop you from moving. A slide has a much smoother surface than grass. The force of friction is much less here, so you slide easily.

▽ Ice is good for sliding, too, because it is very smooth. If you wear ice skates, you can slide even faster. Wheee!

## Fun with magnets

Have you ever played with a magnet? It contains a special kind of force – magnetic force. A magnet attracts many metal objects. It will pick up things like paper clips and nails.

A magnet has two ends, or poles, called north and south. You can see for yourself, if you have two magnets.

Place the two north poles of the magnets together. They will push away from each other. The two south poles together do the same.

But if you put a north pole with a south pole, the magnets attract each other.

The needle of a compass is a magnet. It always points north because the Earth is a magnet, too – a very big one!

## Find out more about . . .

how your muscles pull on pages 12 to 13 (Bones and muscles).

# Simple machines

Do you like doing hard work? Or would you like to find something which makes work easier? Machines do exactly this. A machine is something which works for us. We put a small force into the machine (the force of our muscles) and get a much bigger force out! Machines do not have to be big and complicated. Some are very simple.

## Levers

If you want to lift a heavy weight, use a lever. A lever is a long bar, which rests on a turning point called a pivot. A seesaw is a kind of lever, with the pivot in the middle.

▽ To use a lever, you put one end of it under the weight. Then you push down on the other end. As your end goes down, the end with the weight comes up. The weight needs to be nearer the pivot than you are.

## Wheels

If you want to move a heavy weight a long way, you use wheels. Wheels are round and so they roll easily along the ground. You can join two wheels together with a rod, called an axle.

▽ If you put a box on top of two sets of wheels and axles, you will make a cart! Now you can put the weight in the cart and move it.

## Slopes

A slope made of a flat plank can help you to move a heavy weight upwards. Instead of lifting the weight straight up, you can slide it up the slope. This is much easier!

lever

weight

pivot

## Wedges

One side of a wedge is sharp and thin. The other side is thick. You can easily push the sharp side in between two objects. If you keep on pushing, the thicker part of the wedge gets into the crack. It forces the two objects further apart.

△ An axe is a kind of wedge for splitting wood. A knife is also a wedge. So is a boat! The sharp front of the boat cuts through the water.

## Putting machines together

One simple machine can do only a few jobs. But if you put two or three simple machines together, you can make all sorts of useful machines.

*Find out more about . . .*

other machines on pages 120 to 121 (Machines in action). ▶

▽ A tin opener is made from a wheel (the handle) and a wedge (the cutter).

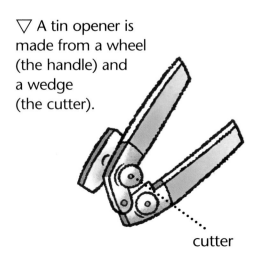

cutter

▽ A wheelbarrow is made from a wheel and two levers (the handles).

▽ Garden shears are made from two levers (the handles) and two wedges (the cutting blades).

# Light and sound

What happens when you wake up in the morning? Perhaps you see the sunlight through your bedroom window?

Perhaps you hear the sound of the alarm clock beside your bed? Different lights and sounds are around us all through the day.

## Light and dark

What can you see in the dark? Of course, you cannot see anything. You need light to see things. Light is a kind of energy. It can travel freely through the air. The Sun gives us light in the daytime. At night, we get light from electric lamps, torches and candles.

△ Switch on a torch in a dark room. A beam of light will shine out from it. If you put your hand in front of the beam, the light does not pass through it. Your hand makes a dark area called a shadow. If you move your hand, the shadow moves too. Can you make shadow shapes on the wall?

◁ When the light from your torch reaches something shiny, it bounces back, or reflects. This is why you can see yourself in a mirror. A mirror is very smooth and shiny. When light from your face reaches the mirror, the light bounces straight back, and you see a picture of yourself.

# Sounds all around

Listen! What sounds can you hear? If you are in a very noisy place, you may hear loud sounds, like the roar of an aircraft or the rat-a-tat of a road drill. If you are in a quiet place, you may hear the ticking of a clock or the buzzing of a fly. So what are sounds? And how are they made?

## Making sounds

Put your hand against your throat. Now hum loudly. You will feel your throat shaking, or vibrating. The vibrations come from the voice box inside your throat. All sounds are made by vibrations like these. A drum vibrates when you hit it. These vibrations make the air around vibrate too. The vibrations in the air are sound waves. They spread out like waves in water.

▷ Sound waves can bounce back – just like beams of light. What happens if you stand in a big empty room and shout? A moment later, you hear your shout again. This is an echo of your voice. The echo is the sound waves from your voice bouncing off the ceiling or walls.

*Find out more about . . .*

eyes and ears
on pages 8 to 9
(Look at me).

sending light and
sound a long way
on pages 124 to 125
(Talking to each other).

musical sounds
on pages 52 to 53
(Music and dance).

# Electricity

Imagine a world without electricity. You would have no television, no freezer, no vacuum cleaner, no electric cooker and no electric light. There would be no telephones and no computers. All of these things are powered by electricity. Electricity is one of the most important kinds of energy in the world.

## Power at home

We use electricity in many ways at home. Electricity can make things work, like the washing machine or the food mixer. It can produce light in a light bulb. It can also produce heat, in an electric cooker or a toaster.

▽ A large city at night is a blaze of light. The power for all these lights comes from electricity.

## Safety first

*Beware! Electricity can be very dangerous. If you touch a bare wire you can get an electric shock. So, NEVER touch electric sockets or plugs. Always ask a grown-up to help you.*

▷ Electric wires are made of metals like copper, because electricity flows easily through them. Electricity cannot flow through plastic, so the wires are usually covered with plastic.

## Electricity goes round

The bulb is not lit. When you connect it with a wire to a battery, the bulb lights up! There is electrical energy inside the battery. This energy flows along the wire to the bulb. Electrical energy will only light the bulb if it is connected in a circle back to the battery. The circle is called a circuit.

copper wire

plastic cover

electricity travels along the wire

the bulb lights up when electricity flows through it

the switch lets you turn the flow of electricity on and off.

electricity is made in the battery

## Power stations

Most of the electricity we use comes from huge buildings called power stations. Here, coal, oil or gas is burned to heat water and make steam. The steam turns giant machines which make electricity flow. This electricity travels along thick wires to factories, shops, schools and homes.

## Find out more about...

how we use electricity on pages 124 and 125 (Talking to each other).

# Using numbers

How many toes do you have? What time is it? How much pocket money have you got left? What was the score in the football match? You use numbers every day, at home and at school. Numbers are very important for other people too. Scientists, builders, bankers, bus drivers, pilots and thousands of other people could not do their jobs without numbers.

▽ How many different ways of using numbers can you spot in this picture?

## One, two, three . . .

It is easy to count up to 10. But have you ever wondered what is so special about 10? To find the answer, you have to go back to the beginning of history. Long ago, some people started counting for the first time by using their fingers. So one set of fingers added up to 10. With fingers, it was easy to take away as well – you just folded a finger down.

### Letters for numbers

*Today, everyone around the world uses the numbers 1, 2, 3, 4, 5, 6, 7, 8, 9, 10. But 2,000 years ago the Romans used letters for different numbers. The Roman numbers for 1 to 10 were I, II, III, IV, V, VI, VII, VIII, IX, X.*

*Some clocks and watches still have Roman numbers on them. See if you can work out from this clock what the Roman numbers for 11 and 12 are.*

# Technology

All the time, scientists are discovering many wonderful things about how our world works. We use their discoveries to make our lives safer and easier. We have fires and fuels to keep us warm. We have machines to carry us around and help us grow food, as well as tools to make and mend things. We have medicines to cure disease. The many ways of using science are part of what we call technology.

# Making materials

Everything around us is made of materials. We can use some materials, such as wood or stone, without changing them very much. But we can also change materials into something very different. We can turn trees into paper, or oil into plastic, or sand into glass. Each of these materials has a different job to do.

tree

wood chips

pulp

## Wool

Wool is a warm and tough material. It grows as a hairy coat called a fleece on sheep, goats and other animals. The fleece is cut off the animal and washed. The tangled fibres of wool are combed straight, then twisted together to make a long thread. This twisting is known as spinning. The wool thread can be woven or knitted to make clothes.

sheep

fleece

combing

pulling

spinning

ball of wool

pulp

rollers

paper

## Paper

Paper is made from wood. The wood from trees is cut into small pieces, or chips. These wood chips are then cooked with chemicals to make the fibres soft. This mixture of cooked wood chips is called pulp. The soggy pulp is laid out and rolled flat. When it is dry, the fibres grow hard again. They stick together to form paper.

paper

plastic

steel

wool

## Something new

To make a new material, you have to start with natural substances. These are called the raw materials. Trees are the raw materials for paper. Rocks are the raw materials for metal. The raw materials are taken to a factory, where they are changed into new materials.

## Iron and steel

Iron is found mixed up with other chemicals in a rock called iron ore. The iron ore is broken up and heated in a huge oven called a blast furnace. The iron part of the ore melts and runs out of the furnace. To make steel from iron, another furnace is used. Steel is much stronger than iron.

iron ore

melted iron

blast furnace

mould

steel furnace

steel ingots

oil

melted plastic

mould

finished bottles

## Plastic

Plastic is light and easy to bend into different shapes. It is made from oil found under the ground. The oil is treated with chemicals to make plastic. When the plastic is heated, it melts into a thick liquid. This can be squashed or moulded into thousands of different shapes.

## New paper from old

*Here is a way to turn old newspapers into your own recycled paper.*

*1. Tear up some sheets of newspaper into bits, and let them soak in a small amount of warm water. Beat up the mixture into a pulp.*

*2. Tip the pulp onto a piece of blotting paper or a tea towel, and spread it out into an even sheet.*

*3. Put more blotting paper or another tea towel over the pulp. Roll it with a rolling pin, then ask a grown-up to iron it. When dry, carefully peel off the blotting paper or tea towels. There is your recycled paper!*

## Find out more about . . . .

oil and metals

on pages 72 to 73

(Rocks, metals and minerals).

# Strong structures

Have you ever been to the top of a tall building? Or travelled through a long, deep tunnel? Or crossed a bridge over a wide valley? Perhaps you wondered how these huge structures were made – and how they stay up! Skyscrapers, tunnels and bridges need to be made of strong materials, like concrete and steel, and they need clever engineers who can make sure that the structures are safe.

## Going up . . .

Some skyscrapers are so tall that they sway in the wind. They must be built so that they can bend, but will not break. Steel and concrete are sunk into the earth to make a steady base for the building. A strong column of concrete is built in the centre of the skyscraper. Then a framework of steel is attached to the column, to hold the floors. The outside of this frame is covered with panels made of light metal and glass.

central core with lifts

steel frame

## Ancient builders

*Long ago, people did not have strong machines or tools. But they could still make amazing structures. About 100,000 workers built the Great Pyramid in Egypt, using over 2 million huge blocks of stone. Even so, it took many years to finish. You can still visit the Great Pyramid today.*

## Going overground

Bridges carry roads and railways over valleys or rivers. Many of the longest are suspension bridges. In a suspension bridge, the roadway hangs from steel cables. The cables are fixed at each end, and are held up by two tall towers.

outside panels

suspension bridge

## Going underground

It is hard to build a road over the top of a mountain, or across a wide river. It is sometimes better to dig a tunnel instead. Engineers often use a special machine for digging tunnels. At the front there are discs which cut away the rock and earth. As the machine moves forward, workers line the tunnel with concrete.

concrete

steel

underground station

*Technology*

# Machines in action

We use machines every day. They help us do an amazing number of things. At home, they clean the clothes, make the toast, play music, wash the dishes and mow the lawn. Big machines like cars and trains carry us from place to place. Even bigger machines help to build buildings and roads. In factories, machines help to make everything from plastic toys to aircraft.

## Super ship

Oil tankers are probably the biggest machines ever made. Some of these ships are so long that they have room for five football pitches on deck!

these pipes bring in hot and cold water

a tiny computer tells the machine when to wash, rinse and spin dry

this cable connects the machine to the electricity supply

detergent goes in here

the clothes go in the drum

this pipe takes away waste water

the motor turns the drum

## Inside a washing machine

How do you wash your clothes? You put them in soapy water. You swirl them about. Then you rinse them with clean water – once, twice, three times. Finally, you squeeze out the water. A washing machine can do all these things – even better than a person. All the machine needs is water, detergent and electricity to make it work.

## Robot worker

Some machines can work
by themselves. We call them
robots. Every move they make
is controlled by a computer.
In car factories, robots help to
put cars together. They do the
more dangerous jobs, such
as welding (joining pieces
of metal by heating them)
and spraying paint.

▽ Most machines are small. But
some are enormous! Some of the
biggest are diggers and trucks. The
digger pulls out the earth with its
bucket. The bucket is big enough
to hold a car! Then the earth is
loaded into the dump truck
and carried away.

## Find out more about...

simple machines
on pages 108 to 109
(Simple machines).

electricity
on pages 112 to 113
(Electricity).

# On the move

How do you get to school each day? You may walk or ride your bike, catch a bus or get a lift in a car. Some children even go to school by boat. If you go on a longer journey, you may travel on an express train, or a jet airliner. Since the very earliest times, people have been inventing bigger, faster and better ways of moving around.

## On foot and on wheels

The first way of moving was on foot. People carried their belongings on their back. Later on, they invented carts pulled by animals to move heavy weights.

horse and cart

**Montgolfier balloon**

### Balloons

The first aircraft to fly was a balloon, built by two brothers, called Montgolfier. On board were a sheep, a chicken and a duck!

"The Rocket"

### Steam trains

About 300 years ago, people discovered that trucks with heavy loads could be pulled along more easily on rails than on roads. The earliest railway engines were driven by steam.

### Paddles and sails

Early boats wer pushed through the water using poles or paddles. Sailing ships harnessed the power of the wind to move them along.

sailing ship

ocean liner

Wright flyer

early
jet fighter

# Technology

Space
Shuttle

## From propellors to jets

The first aeroplane was also built by two brothers – the Wright brothers. It was driven along by propellers. Modern aircraft have jet engines. Gases from burning fuel shoot out of the engines, pushing the aircraft forwards.

## Rockets

Spacecraft use rocket engines. These are special because they are the only engines that work out in space.

## Bicycles

Bicycles have always had two wheels, but some early models were very hard to ride. They had a huge front wheel, and a tiny back one.

TGV

## Cars

The first motor car had only three wheels. It had no roof, and hard seats. Modern cars have four wheels, and are roomy and comfortable.

people carrier

penny-
farthing

## The fastest train

Today's trains have diesel engines, or are powered by electricity. The fastest train in the world is the French high-speed train, the TGV.

## Modern ships

hydrofoil

Big modern ships have diesel engines that are powered by burning oil. They can carry very heavy loads a long way. Most boats float part in, part out of the water. However, submarines travel underwater, while hovercraft and hydrofoils skim along the surface.

## Find out more about . . .

gravity and why things move on pages 106 to 107 (Motion and force).

wheels and axles on pages 108 to 109 (Simple machines).

# Talking to each other

When you are sitting at home, it is easy to pick up the telephone and talk to a friend far away. You can switch on the television and watch a game of basketball in a foreign country. You can turn on the radio and hear music. Telephones, televisions and radios can bring messages into your home from all over the world.

## Sending signals

Everyone wants to watch the Olympic Games. They are watched on television by millions of people – all at the same time. Television engineers send signals from television cameras all round the world in an instant.

satellite

$\triangleright$ First, the pictures of the runners have to be changed into electric signals. The camera does this. The signals travel down a wire to a satellite dish.

satellite dish

electric signals

$\triangleleft$ The satellite dish turns the electric signals into radio signals, and sends them to a satellite high above the Earth.

camera

## Waves through the air

▽ The satellite passes on the radio signals to another satellite dish on a TV station on the other side of the world. A transmitter sends them on to your TV at home.

The signals that reach your radio or television do not travel along wires all the way to your home. They travel part of the way through the air, just like waves of sound. They are called radio signals. Thousands and sometimes millions of these signals reach your radio every second.

## ! Cardboard TV

*The very first television set was made by a man called John Logie Baird in 1924. He used all sorts of things to build it. These included sheets of cardboard, knitting needles, a biscuit tin and sealing wax!*

television station

transmitter

TV set

## On the phone

You cannot talk to a radio or a television, but a telephone is different. It sends messages both ways – out from your home, and in from the people who phone you. When you speak into the mouthpiece of a telephone, your words are turned into an electric signal. The signal travels down the wire to your friend. The voice of your friend travels back to you in just the same way.

△ Your television changes the signals back into pictures and sounds.

## Find out more about . . .

sound waves on page 111 (Light and sound).

how we make and use electricity on pages 112 to 113 (Electricity).

# Great inventions

For over two million years, people have been inventing things. An invention might be a tool, a machine or a way of using a material. But it has to be something new. Most inventions, such as medicines, have helped us. But not all inventions have been useful. Some, such as guns and bombs, have caused a lot of harm.

**Plough**
Early farmers sowed their seeds in holes made with a stick. Then about 8,000 years ago, farmers made the first ploughs, out of pointed branches. With ploughs they could sow more quickly and grow much more food.

**Electric light**
The first reliable electric light bulbs were invented in the 1870s. Electric light was much better than flickering oil or gas lamps.

**Tinned food**
About 200 years ago, a Frenchman discovered that if he sealed food in a container, it lasted for a very long time without spoiling. Sailors and other travellers could now carry food on long journeys without it going rotten.

**Telephone**
Telephones were invented in the USA at around the same time as electric light. For the first time people could talk to each other when they were hundreds of kilometres apart!

**Bicycle**
Early bicycles were not very fast or comfortable, but in 1885 a new design called the 'safety cycle' was built. This was the first modern bicycle. Today bicycles are used all over the world, wherever people need a cheap way of getting about.

### Wheel
People first began to use wheels in the Middle East about 3,500 years ago. They put wheels on carts, and used potter's wheels for making pottery. They also made waterwheels.

### Gunpowder
The Chinese invented gunpowder about 1,000 years ago by mixing charcoal with other chemicals. It was used to fire cannonballs and bullets, and to make fireworks.

### Steam engine
The earliest steam engines were built about 250 years ago. They were used to power all sorts of machines, and later to drive steam trains and steamships. Petrol engines, jets and other kinds of engine could not have been invented without the steam engine.

### Telescope
A telescope is really two magnifying lenses, one at each end of a long tube. It makes things that are far away look much closer. The first ones were made nearly 400 years ago in the Netherlands.

### Plastic
In 1911 a Belgian scientist made a new kind of material called bakelite. It was the first plastic. Many other kinds of plastic soon followed. Now plastics are used to make everything from clothing to high-speed aircraft.

### Computer
The earliest computers were built about 50 years ago. They were huge, because they had big glass valves instead of tiny microchips. Today's computers can do all sorts of jobs, from forecasting the weather to playing games.

# Computers

We build most machines to do one special job. An electric drill makes holes. A hairdryer dries your hair. A clock tells you the time. But a computer can do lots of jobs. It can do sums and it can store information. It can help you to write letters and to draw plans. It does all these things using tiny electronic circuits called "microchips".

## Computers at work

We tell a computer what to do by typing on the keyboard or by clicking the mouse. The computer can do what we ask because it has a set of instructions called a program stored on microchips inside it. There are many kinds of program, and each one has a different set of instructions.

▽ Some programs work with words and numbers. Banks, shops and office workers use these programs.

△ Other programs work with drawings and plans. Engineers and designers use these programs.

△ Computer games are another kind of program. You might have some on a computer at home or at school.

## Hidden computers

Lots of the things that we use every day have a computer inside them. This is a computer, even though it does not look like one! Inside this video camera is a tiny computer, which controls the way the camera works.

## Books on chips

*Computers can store enormous amounts of information on one tiny microchip. All the words and pictures in this encyclopedia can be stored on a chip the same size as your fingertip!*

# The Universe

The Universe is everything out in space.
Nobody knows how big the Universe is.
To us, the Earth seems huge. Yet the Earth
is only a small planet that travels around
the Sun. The Sun itself is a star. If you look
at the sky on a clear night, you can see
thousands and thousands of other stars.
In the vast space of the Universe, the Earth
and the Sun are only tiny specks!

△ The Earth is one of nine
planets that move round
the Sun. And the Sun is just
one of the millions of stars
in the enormous Universe.

# The Sun and the Moon

The Earth is a planet that travels round the Sun. We say that the Earth orbits the Sun. It takes one year (about 365 days) to go all the way round. At the same time the Moon orbits the Earth. It takes about 28 days for the Moon to go right round the Earth. The Moon is our nearest neighbour in space.

## A ball of gases

The Sun is a giant ball of very hot, glowing gases. They are squeezed together so tightly that the centre of the Sun is unbelievably hot. The heat flows up to the surface and then out into space. Only a tiny part of the Sun's heat and light reach us on Earth. Even these are so powerful that you should never look directly at the Sun.

◁ Dark patches sometimes appear on the surface of the Sun. These patches are sunspots. They are areas where the surface is cooler and less bright than the rest of the Sun. A large sunspot can be bigger than the whole of the planet Earth!

### Find out more about . . .

day and night
on pages 70 to 71
(Climates and seasons).

the Sun's energy
on pages 104 to 105
(Everything needs energy).

## No life

There is no air or water on the Moon. In fact there is no life there at all. The Moon is just a ball of rock covered with dust. On its surface there are mountains and big holes called craters.

Moon

Earth

## Phases of the Moon

Why does the Moon shine? It has no light of its own. All the Moon's light comes from the Sun. It is then reflected down to us on Earth. The Sun's rays always light up half of the Moon's surface. At the same time the other half is in darkness. But as the Moon travels round the Earth, we see different amounts of its bright side. It seems as if the Moon is slowly changing shape all the time. These different shapes are called the phases of the Moon.

▽ The Moon takes 28 days to go through all these phases.

| full Moon | three-quarter Moon | half Moon | crescent Moon | Moon completely hidden |

# The planets

The Earth and eight other planets are all whizzing round the Sun. We call the Sun and its family of planets the Solar System. (The word solar means "of the Sun".) All nine planets in the Solar System are kept in their place by the pull of gravity. The Sun's gravity tugs on them and stops them flying off into outer space.

## Nearest to furthest

All the planets in the Solar System orbit the Sun at different distances. Mercury is the nearest – and one of the hottest! Venus is next closest, and it is hot there, too. Next nearest the Sun is the Earth. Beyond the Earth are Mars, Jupiter, Saturn, Uranus, Neptune and, furthest away of all, Pluto.

Neptune

Pluto

Jupiter

Sun

Earth

Venus

Uranus

Mars

Mercury

Saturn

## Big and small

The planets in the Solar System are all different sizes. The Sun is bigger than any of them – it is over 100 times wider than the Earth. The planets are shown below in their order from the Sun.

△ This picture shows all the planets in the Solar System orbiting round the Sun.

▽ Mercury is one of the smallest planets. It is bare and rocky.

▽ Venus is the brightest planet in the night sky. It is covered in poisonous gases.

▽ Earth looks blue from space because so much of the surface is water.

▽ Mars is an orangey-red colour. This is because of the dust storms that blow across it.

▽ Jupiter is the biggest planet. It is mainly made of gas, but there are liquids and rock deep inside it.

## Shooting stars

Have you ever seen a sudden streak of light in the sky? It was probably a shooting star. Shooting stars are not stars at all. Lots of small pieces of rock are flying around the Solar System. Some of them rush straight towards the Earth. When they reach the atmosphere, the rocks become very hot and burn up. This burning is what you see in the sky.

## Amazing space!

*If planes could fly through space, we could fly right across the Solar System. But it would take a very long time! The Solar System is so huge that even Concorde, which flies faster than the speed of sound, would take 500 years to fly right across!*

## Find out more about . . .

the forces of friction and gravity on pages 106 to 107 (Pushing and pulling).

why stars twinkle on pages 134 to 135 (The stars).

▽ Saturn has rings around it. These are made of lots of separate pieces of ice.

▽ Uranus also has rings. It was the first planet to be discovered by someone using a telescope.

▽ Neptune is so far from the Sun that it takes 165 years to go right round. It has a ring, too.

▽ Pluto is on the edge of the Solar System. It was only discovered about 70 years ago.

# The stars

Have you ever tried counting the stars? It is a very difficult thing to do. There are thousands of them! Even if you could count all the stars you can see, there are millions more that you cannot see without a telescope. Every one of these stars is a glowing ball of gas, just like our Sun.

△ This cloud of gas out in space is called the Crab Nebula. One day in the future, it may become a star.

### How a star is made

Where do stars come from? Out in space, there are clouds of dust and gas between the stars. As these clouds move along, they pull more dust and gas towards them. The gas is crushed tightly into a ball, and becomes very, very hot. The star is a bit like a giant power station, giving out lots of heat and light.

### The Milky Way

Stars are not scattered evenly through space. They come together in enormous star groups, called galaxies. Our Sun is part of a galaxy called the Milky Way. You can easily see the Milky Way on a clear night. It stretches in a misty band right across the sky.

## Shapes in the sky

If you look carefully, you can see that some bright stars make shapes in the sky. The shapes can look like animals, or like people. They have names too. There is a Great Bear and a Little Bear, a Dragon, a Scorpion and a Dog.

▽ If you live in the northern half of the world, one of the easiest star shapes to see is Orion the Hunter. You can find it by spotting three bright stars in a row – these are Orion's belt. (You can only see Orion in the winter.)

▷ If you live in the southern half of the world, you will always be able to see the Southern Cross in the night sky. Its four bright stars make the shape of a cross.

## Why do stars twinkle?

When you look at a star in the sky, it seems to twinkle. In fact, the star is giving out steady beams of light. This light has to travel a very long way through space to reach us. Then it has to pass through the Earth's atmosphere, the layer of moving air that surounds our planet. The air bends and breaks up the star's beams of light - and that makes the light twinkle.

*Find out more about . . .*

gravity on
pages 106 to 107
(Forces and movement).

# Exploring space

The Universe is a very mysterious place. We have started to explore just our own tiny corner of it. Spacecraft with people on board have landed on the Moon.

Other people have spent many weeks inside space stations going round the Earth. Spacecraft with nobody on board have travelled much farther – right to the edge of the Solar System.

## Into the unknown

For centuries, people have dreamed of travelling in space. Yet that dream has only come true in the past 50 years. These are some of the important events in space exploration.

fuel tank ....     rocket booster

△ Most spacecraft are used only once. But the Space Shuttle can be used again and again. When it takes off, the Shuttle has a huge fuel tank and two rocket boosters attached to it. When the fuel runs out, these break away and fall back to Earth.

1957  Sputnik, the first spacecraft, went into orbit round the Earth.

1969  Apollo 11 landed the first people on the Moon. They were two American astronauts.

1976  Two Viking space probes landed on Mars, and sent back pictures of the planet's surface.

## A record stay in space

People can now live in space for a long time. The record-holder is a Russian spaceman who spent 438 days (well over a year) on board the space station Mir.

## Walking in space

camera

Astronauts sometimes have to work outside their spacecraft. They wear a special suit with its own supply of oxygen so they can breathe. The backpack is really a tiny jet engine. The astronauts use it to move around outside the spacecraft.

backpack

△ We can look at space through telescopes. But the dust and winds in the Earth's atmosphere get in the way. In 1990, scientists sent a telescope up into space to get a clearer look. It is called the Hubble Space Telescope. It sends us amazing pictures of faraway stars and galaxies.

1986  The Russian space station Mir (which means "peace") went into orbit. It is still in space, and extra parts have been added on.

1989 The space probe Voyager 2 flew past Neptune. Earlier on, it had passed Jupiter, Saturn and Uranus.

1995 The spacecraft Galileo reached Jupiter. It sent a small probe into Jupiter's atmosphere to take close-up pictures.

# Glossary

**artery** a tube or vessel which carries blood away from the heart.

**astronaut** a person who flies in a spacecraft.

**axis** a straight line around which something turns.

**bacteria** very simple creatures made of a single cell. Some bacteria cause disease.

**battery** a source of electricity that is portable.

**biceps** the large muscle in the upper arm, which flexes the elbow.

**bone marrow** soft tissue inside your bones, where new blood cells are made.

**carbon dioxide** a gas in the air. When we breathe out, we get rid of unwanted carbon dioxide from our bodies. It is also produced when something burns or rots.

**cell** tiny parts from which all living things are made.

**chickenpox** an illness where you have itchy spots on the skin and a high temperature.

**concrete** a mixture of water, sand, cement and gravel, which sets hard to make a strong material for building.

**dermis** the living part of the skin, which is below the outer level, or epidermis.

**desert** an area where hardly any rain falls. Few plants and animals can live there, because it is so dry.

**detergent** a cleaning substance that helps to lift dirt and grease off things that need cleaning.

**diaphragm** a large muscle below the lungs, between the chest and the lower body. It helps with breathing.

**digestion** the process which breaks down food in our stomachs, so that it can be used in the body.

**epidermis** the outer layer of the skin.

**fasting** not eating food, usually for religious reasons.

**fibres** thin strands or threads.

**fossil** the remains of a plant or animal from long ago. Many fossils are found inside rocks.

**fuel** something which is used up to produce energy, for example by burning it.

**fungus** a kind of plant that cannot make food using air and sunlight. Mushrooms are one type of fungus.

**germ** a tiny living creature, which can cause disease.

**gill** the "lungs" of water-living animals, which allow them to breathe.

**gravity** the force that pulls objects towards the Earth.

**grub** a fat, worm-like creature. The young of insects are grubs.

**gullet** the throat.

**hurricane** a violent storm with heavy rain and very strong winds.

**intestine** part of the digestive system that connects to the stomach.

**junk** a flat-bottomed boat used in China and the Far East.

**kidneys** the organs which help to take waste materials out of the blood.

**lens** a piece of curved glass that bends light. Some lenses make things look bigger.

**ligament** a band of fibres connecting bones or muscles.

**liver** the organ in the body which helps to make blood and process food.

**melanin** a dark colouring found in the skin.

**mineral** a type of substance found in the ground, such as oil or coal.

**mould** a hollow shape into which a liquid is poured. The liquid then sets in the shape of the mould.

**muscle** a bundle of fibres in the body which tighten or relax to move parts of the body.

**nectar** a sweet liquid made by flowers.

**nerves** thin fibres that carry electrical messages to and from the brain.

**ore** a rock which is rich in one type of metal

**oxygen** a gas in the air, which we need to breathe to stay alive.

**pollen** a fine powder produced by flowers so that they can create seeds.

**pores** tiny holes in the skin of an animal, which let out sweat and help to keep it cool.

**propeller** a shaft with blades, which turns to push a boat or aircraft along.

**rainforest** a thick tropical forest, where a lot of rain falls all year round.

**rocket** a type of flying machine that is pushed along at high speed by a jet of hot gases.

**satellite** a moon or a spacecraft that circles around a planet.

**shrine** a place devoted to a holy person or object.

**skyscraper** a building so tall that it seems to "scrape the sky".

**spinal cord** the bundle of nerves that is protected by the bones of the spine.

**staple food** the most important food grown or eaten in a region.

**stethoscope** an instrument for listening to sounds inside the body.

**tadpole** a young frog or toad, which can only live in water.

**termite** an insect like an ant, which lives in large colonies.

**trawler** a kind of fishing boat that catches fish in a large net pulled behind it.

**urine** liquid carrying waste material from the body.

**uterus** the place inside the body of female mammals where babies develop.

**vein** a tube or vessel which carries blood to the heart.

# Index

# Acknowledgements

## Illustrations

cover Julian Baum/Jonatronics; icons Alan (Fred) Pipes; 2 Benedict Blaythwayt; 4 t Michael Courtney; 4 c Ellen Beier; 4 b Scot Ritchie; 5 cl Sean Milne; 5 br Oxford Illustrators; 7 Clive Goodyer; 7 b, 8 b Michael Courtney; 8 t, 9 t Scot Ritchie; 9 cr, 10 b Michael Courtney; 10 t Julie Park; 10 c Scot Ritchie; 11 tl Lynne Willey; 11 tr Scot Ritchie; 12 t Michael Courtney; 12 b Lynne Willey/Steve Weston; 13 t Clive Goodyer; 14 Lynne Willey/Steve Weston; 15 tl Steve Weston/Clive Goodyer; 15 bl, bc Lynne Willey; 15 br Scot Ritchie; 16 b, 17 t Clive Goodyer; 17 b Lynne Willey; 18, 19c Clive Goodyer; 19 t, bl, bc, br Scot Ritchie; 20–21 Clive Goodyer; 22–23 Michael Courtney; 23 tr Scot Ritchie; 24–25 Scot Ritchie; 25 tl Lynne Willey; 26 b Lynne Willey; 27 tl Scot Ritchie; 27 b, 28 t Lynne Willey; 28 c Clive Goodyer; 28 b Scot Ritchie; 29 Georgie Birkett; 30, 31 br Scot Ritchie; 32 bl, bc, br, 33 bl, bc Julian Baker; 33 cr Scot Ritchie; 34–35 Benedict Blaythwayt; 36–37 Georgie Birkett; 38–39 Annabel Spenceley; 38 bl Andrea Norton; 39 cr, br Scot Ritchie; 41 l Steve Lach; 41 r Scot Ritchie; 42, 43, 44, 45, 46, 47 Ellen Beier; 44, 45, 46, 47 (globes) Julian Baker; 48–49 Chris Brown; 50 Ellen Beier; 50 (globes) Julian Baker; 51 Louise Harker; 52–53 Annabel Spenceley; 53 tr, cr, br Scot Ritchie; 54–55 Annabel Spenceley; 54 t, 55 tl, tr, cr, br, 56 c, bl, br Georgie Birkett; 57 r Scot Ritchie; 58 t Ellen Beier; 58 bl Tessa Eccles; 58 br Scot Ritchie; 59 Julian Baum; 60–61 Oxford University Press Cartographic Department; 62 Julian Baum; 62 tr Scot Ritchie; 63 b Julian Baum; 65 bl Michael Eaton; 65 tr Scot Ritchie; 66–67 Steve Lings; 67 br, 68 tr Scot Ritchie; 68–69 Steve Lings; 69 br Peter Joyce; 70–71 Oxford University Press Cartographic Department; 71 br, 72 cl, c, cr, 73 b Chris Brown; 73 tl, tr Scot Ritchie; 74 l John Haslam; 74 r Peter Visscher; 75 Michael Strand; 76 l John Davies; 76 r Linden Artists; 77 cl, c Peter Visscher; 77 cr Tim Halliday; 77 bl Scot Ritchie; 78–79 Peter Visscher; 78–79 (background) Julian Baker; 80, 81 cr Terry Riley; 81 bl Scot Ritchie; 82–83 John Davies; 83 cr Scot Ritchie; 84–85, 84 cl, b, 85 bl John Butler; 85 br Scot Ritchie; 86–87 Sean Milne; 87 br Scot Ritchie; 88–89, 89 cr John Butler; 89 br Scot Ritchie; 90–91, 90 t Steve Roberts; 91 tr Scot Ritchie; 92–93, 94–95 John Butler; 96–97 Brinn Edwards; 98 Steve Roberts; 99 Clive Goodyer; 100 bc, br, 101 tr Scot Ritchie; 102 bl Clive Goodyer; 102 tr Joshua Smith; 103 l Lynne Willey; 104–105 Annabel Spenceley; 105 tr Scot Ritchie; 105 cr Clive Goodyer; 107 t, bl Scot Ritchie; 107 cr Tessa Eccles; 107 br Alan Fred Pipes; 108 b Scot Ritchie; 108–109 Scot Ritchie; 109 t Scot Ritchie; 109 b Clive Goodyer; 110 t Lynne Willey; 110 b, 111 b Scot Ritchie; 111 tl Lynne Willey; 111 tr, 112 tr, 113 t Clive Goodyer; 114 Scot Ritchie; 115, 116-117 Clive Goodyer; 116 br Lynne Willey; 117 r, 118 b Scot Ritchie; 118–119 Benedict Blaythwayt; 120 t Scot Ritchie; 120 b Oxford Illustrators; 121 b Andy Burton; 122–123 Georgia Birkett; 124–125 Clive Goodyer; 124 b Doug Gray; 125 cr Doug Gray; 126–127 Georgie Birkett; 128 br Scot Ritchie; 128 cl, c, cr Joshua Smith; 129, 130–131, 132–133 Julian Baum; 133 tr Scot Ritchie; 134–135 Ellen Beier/Julian Baum; 135 tr Julian Baum; 136–137 Julian Baum; 136 Julian Baum; 137 tl Oxford Illustrators.

## Photographs

The publishers would like to thank the following for permission to reproduce photographs:
Title page Harding (R. Behrmann); 5 t SPL (K. Wood); 5 c SPL (D. Parker); 5 b SPL (Dr J. Burgess); 9 tr Image Bank (Gary Chapman); 11 br OUP; 11 bl OUP; 13 b SPL (J. Wachter); 15 tr SPL (M. Clarke); 16 tr SPL (A. Polliack); 22 cl SPL (D. Fawcett); 23 br Harding (Dr D. K. Holdsworth); 26 t SPL (A. B. Dowsett); 27 tr SPL (J.-L. Charmet); 31 t Sally & Richard Greenhill; 31 b Latha Menon; 32 —33 Lifefile (J. Hoare); 40 Image Bank (P. J. Lacroix); 56 t Sally & Richard Greenhill; 57 l Eon Productions/United Artists; 63 tr Harding (R. Behrmann); 64 —65 SPL (Krafft Explorer); 65 br Harding (T. Waltham); 67 tr Image Bank (S. Wilkinson); 69 tr SPL (K. Wood); 70 t Image Bank (J. du Boisberrai); 70 b NHPA (A. Mardi); 71 t Harding (Roy Rainford); 71 bl Bryan & Cherry Alexander (Ann Hawthorne); 71 c NHPA (M. Harvey); 72 bl, bc, br, 73 t Geoscience Features (Dr B. Booth); 77 t NHPA (Stephen Dalton); 81 t Corbis Images (Sally Morgan); 82 l NHPA (M. Leach); 83 tr Planet Earth (Y. Shibner); 91 bl Image Bank (M. Mead); 95 t NHPA (J. Shaw); 96 b NHPA (P. Parks); 98 World Wide Fund for Nature; 100 t NHPA (Kevin Schafer); 101 b SPL (TEK Image); 102 c SPL (D. J. Burgess); 103 r De Beers; 106 t, b Action Plus (G. Kirk); 112 b Harding (N. Francis); 113 b SPL (M. Bond); 121 t SPL (D. Parker); 125 tr; Getty Images 128 bl Sony UK; 134 t Julian Baum/NASA; 136 tr SPL (NASA); 137 tr SPL (NASA).

Abbreviations: Harding = Robert Harding Picture Library ; NHPA = Natural History Photographic Agency; OUP = Oxford University Press; SPL = Science Photo Library.